The Life of a
Paramedic And God

Knocking on Heaven's Door

Shane Turvey

ISBN: 9798845688590
Imprint: Independently published (paperback)

Also available as a Kindle e-book and hardback

Contents

Foreword Justin Prangnell
Acknowledgements and Dedication
Introduction and Caveat

Chapter:
1   In the Beginning   1
2   Millennium   7
3   Choking *'Heimlich Manoeuvre'* ROSC a thump
     and a   knock on the head   19
4   Death Experience   27
5   The Right to Die   33
6   Dying, the Hospice and Healing   40
7   Anecdotes   51
8   Average Days   60
9   A Not so Average Day   72
10 Contaminated Blood   83
11 Terror and Worst Year   88
12 Covid-19, King Arthur and Hope   97
13 Step into Eternity with God   106

Appendix 1: Science and religion   111
Appendix 2: Driver training syllabus   115
Glossary   124
References   126

Foreword

by Justin Prangnell

If you have ever wondered what it's like to be a frontline NHS paramedic, then this book is for you. It offers a 'no holds barred' approach into the things you experience in this role, as well as the toll it takes on individuals that follow this career path. It is full of real life incidents that will make you laugh and cry at times.

When I first met Shane (author) outside the Two Shires ambulance HQ 22 years ago, I never would have believed we would become great friends and even share holidays together with our families. Shane was heavily involved with meditation, martial arts and healing crystals. We were an unlikely match as friends, considering our differing beliefs. I have never been overly 'overt' in my Christian faith but I found myself working with a person that asked me many questions such as "don't all religions essentially worship the same God?" this was in-between attending 999 calls! Shane explains his amazing journey to faith in this book and I feel immensely proud to have played a very small part in it.

Justin Prangnell Operations Officer, South Western Ambulance Service NHS Foundation Trust

Acknowledgements and Dedication

I write this book with great indebtedness to all the known and undisclosed patients I have attended, most of whom trusted their care to me, as strangers in a time of great distress. Their stories in this book have impacted me deeply in so many ways for more than two decades. I hope I have conveyed their experiences in a way that is not flippant, but real and honest.

I wish to acknowledge the dedication of my ambulance colleagues, for their professionalism, commitment and hard work, and for their support, friendship and camaraderie.

I would like to thank Ann Kenny for her honesty, encouragement and gift of her time spent reading and editing this work.

I must thank my awesome and beautiful wife Debbie, who is the single best person I know. It has always been you; I love you more than words can express. Thank you, Scott, Chloe and Emily, my children, for being such beautiful and caring people and for being in my life, I love you all dearly.

I thank my dad for his lifelong friendship, guidance, being my go-to person in difficult times, and being a rock to stand on. I thank my heavenly Father for His leading, Grace and Forgiveness.

Joseph Benjamin Huitson

28.12.1966 – 10.06.2021

Introduction and Caveat

If you would like to work for the ambulance service or are just curious as to what ambulance staff experience, know and do, then this book is written for you. If you are a Christian and would like to know how trauma and death is shaped when walking with God, or perhaps you would like to believe there is a God, then this book is written for you also.

The stories in this book are real. Some personal details have been changed to protect identity and confidentiality where necessary, some names given are those involved, and they have granted permission to use them. *Caveat*: If you are offended by death or easily upset then do not read this book for obvious reasons - it is about trauma and death encountered by ambulance service personnel. If the Christian faith offends you, this book is also about God. It is not written to offend anyone; it is written to offer hope. It is unashamedly also about faith in Jesus.

This book is packed with events many of which are shocking. This work includes some of the worst incidents I have attended. It is written from my own real experience as a paramedic with more than 23 years on the NHS emergency service front line. I believe that some of the material in this book will challenge what you know and believe. It also contains material that 99% of the population has not witnessed, not even many GP's.

The Ambulance Service specialises in saving lives and caring for the sick and broken, as well as each other – we hopefully enable people to stay safe. Christians aspire to be like Jesus, healing the sick and caring for the lost, the last and the least.

Pause for thought: For whoever would save his life will lose it, but whoever loses his life for my sake will find it - Mat 16:25

Chapter 1- In the Beginning

I first joined 'Two Shires' NHS Ambulance Service on Wednesday 14th October 1998, two weeks before my 32nd birthday and four weeks before taking a black belt in Shotokan Karate, something which I will talk more on later. Two Shires ambulance service was an amalgamation in 1993 of the Buckinghamshire and Northamptonshire ambulance services. My initial ambulance service training consisted of a 4 day first aid course, a residential six weeks trainee ambulance technician programme, awarded by the Institute of Health Care Development (IHCD) and four weeks emergency driver training including a skidpan day at Silverstone racing circuit (see appendix 2).

Before my ambulance service career began, I had previously had three significant periods of unemployment. This was a difficult time for me having three young children, Scott age 5, Chloe age 4 and Emily just 10 months old. My self-esteem was at an all-time low and I was struggling to make ends meet, in fact I had run up large debts. I had hit rock bottom and could not predict how a career in the ambulance service would change my life in so many ways. Leading up to this it was winter 1997 and Emily was just a baby in arms when my wife Debbie and I had noticed she appeared unwell. We called the night duty doctor who eventually made a home visit and diagnosed a throat infection. Later that same morning I took the family food shopping and as I carried Emily through the supermarket in my arms, I began to have real concerns about her appearance. At that time, I had no clinical training but knew something was very wrong. Her eyes lacked lustre and the whites of her eyes had greyness to them. Her skin was clammy, and she was unusually quiet and inactive. I listened to that inner voice telling me she was sick and said to Debbie that we were abandoning our already filled shopping trolley in the aisle and

1

were taking Emily straight to hospital. Debbie agreed without hesitation.

What I had subconsciously done was what I now know as the paediatric assessment triangle (PAT), a tool used by emergency clinicians to make a rapid initial assessment of a sick child. This uses visual tools of observing appearance, work of breathing and circulation to skin. My experience as a paramedic over the years has shown me to listen carefully to concerned parents who have an intuition. Parents know when something is wrong with their child, even if it is not easily put into words. Emily had very low oxygen saturations (SpO2) at the emergency department and the night duty doctor who had seen her earlier that morning had missed double pneumonia, an infection on both lungs normally caused by a viral infection in small children. This had made her very unwell. Emily spent several days in Stoke Mandeville hospital and we were blessed to take her home Christmas Eve December 1997.

A couple of years before joining the ambulance service I had previously trained as a prison officer, joining Her Majesties prison service. After 10 months of stress, feeling sick with worry and dread, I knew this was not the career for me. I phoned in one morning and said I that would not be returning. This was another period of unemployment I had entered and my decision to leave my job left me unable to make the mortgage payments on our home. It was now early 1998 and I thought long and hard about my future. Could I join the ambulance service, and would I be happy there? Would my application be rejected because I hadn't completed my first year of probation with the prison service? Could I help the sick and injured and how would I respond to seeing terrible injuries? At this time unemployment was very high and there would be many other applicants. I decided that I had nothing to lose and made an application and was delighted when I was invited to attend a full day of assessments on Friday 27th February 1998. The day included a driving assessment, a fitness test, a dexterity test, an aptitude test, group work and I was also required to make a 3-minute presentation on a subject of my choice. My talk was on the saxophone, a lifelong passion of mine. If all this went well it would be followed by an interview on 04.03.98.

Overall, I am a naturally quiet person and some people perceive this as being really laid back. One thing that I felt would go against me at interview was a real fear I had of public speaking. Arriving at the ambulance station I remember feeling sick with nerves. I just needed to do my best and hope for a little luck too. I was greeted by Elspeth, a member of the HR team and remember feeling very welcomed by her. I was led to the bottom games room the ambulance crews used and waited there with the other applicants. There was a pool table, a darts board, a TV and a green sofa. Some of the other applicants seemed to ooze confidence and were talking about emergency driving and ambulance aid as if they knew everything about it. I started to feel even more out of my depth. We all took the tests and a dictation exam and then it was time for the 3-minute presentation. I had rehearsed this over and over and felt sure about what I wanted to say. It went well but I didn't know if the assessment panel could see how nervous I was. This was then followed with a group activity and again I was feeling very nervous. I am not an assertive person; had I participated enough in the activity and was I seen as being a team player?

A few days later and I arrived back at the ambulance station for an interview, however this did not go as well as I had hoped, and I thought I had blown it. I had totally misconstrued a question when asked what duties I thought an ambulance person might do. I thought I was being asked about *station* duties such as cleaning the vehicle or restocking equipment, but the question was about what kind of *incidents* I might be expected to attend. Fortunately, I was pressed further and eventually responded with the right answers. After what felt like a painful interview, I went home thinking I had very little chance. To my delight, a few days later I would discover that I would embark on a career that is like no other. The highs would be stratospheric, and the lows are like staring into the abyss. No two days are ever the same and it is impossible to exhaust all the possible scenarios that you could be exposed to. Ambulance work includes attending emergency cases of accident, acute and chronic illness and sudden death. There are GP urgent admissions, special and planned patient journeys including intensive care transfers, maternity incidents and the delivery of babies, cardiac arrests, mental health crisis, social needs, self-harm, assaults, the deceased, infectious diseases, emergency driving and so much more. All these things and much more will be covered by this book.

In 1998 my starting salary was £9,511 per annum being 80% pay of a fully qualified ambulance technician's pay. Trainees were known as 80 'percent-ers' until qualified. My first month's pay packet was £704.09. At that time, there were only two grades of ambulance clinician, ambulance technicians and paramedics. You were required to complete a minimum of a year as a trainee ambulance technician before qualifying. After this, if selected you could further apply to join a paramedic IHCD training programme. To do this you were required to pass an entrance exam. In 1998 there was no central professional body of registration for paramedics. A professional national register would later be introduced in 2000. Since that time, it has been mandatory for paramedics to register with the Health and Care Professions Council (HCPC).

The in-service training course was residential during the academic and practical training period of six weeks, staying at a local hotel Monday through Thursday and travel back home Friday afternoon. All food and drink were catered for. The modern paramedic's training today has moved away from this kind of in-house objective-based courses to more academic and evidence-based practice delivered by universities at degree level (Bachelor of Science Honours) level. However, this isn't the only route into the ambulance service and some services currently offer an apprenticeship. You can also become an

ECA (emergency care assistant). You are also required to have a C1 driving license and pass the emergency driver training.

Pause for thought:
What makes up the so called 'simple' cell? [1]*Each cell in the human body contains more information than all 30 volumes of Encyclopaedia Britannica. There are approximately 37 trillion cells in the human body each cell containing some 42 million protein molecules.*

My first shift out on the road was a night shift on 26th December 1998 working out of Amersham ambulance station, Buckinghamshire. Back then shifts were 8 hours long, this one starting at 23:00 and finishing 07:00am. This small ambulance station looked from the outside more like a fire station, than what I had imagined an ambulance station might look like. All that was missing was a pole to slide down to the ambulance garages below. The station front consisted of three green roller garage doors behind which the ambulances were parked, which were beneath the upstairs crew rooms and kitchen. At the top of the concrete stairs you took to get above the bays was a small stores room. As you entered right into the first crew room there stood a full-sized snooker table and a cocktail version of the original space invaders game developed by Tomohiro Nishikado in the 1970's. To the right was the locker room and straight ahead the team leader's office and a second crew room for relaxing. The kitchen and W/C's were off to the left of the first crew room.

I was greeted by my crew mate Sue Redman, who was a qualified ambulance technician. She was very welcoming as did her best to reassure me and put me at ease for my first ever shift on the road. Back then as now, there was a national shortage of paramedics. We were a double ambulance technician crew, both being clinical but neither of us having extended paramedic skills. As my first 'emergency' came in I remember feeling nervous. The base station radio bleep activated, a high-pitched sound that slightly startled you, and

5

then the controller would pass some basic information about the incoming incident. The shift was steady, but most of the incidents we attended were not really 'emergencies' in the true sense. I survived my first shift and was home in bed by 08:00am.

A few weeks soon came and went without anything significant happening. However, within only two months of the start of my career I would attend a cot death in Milton Keynes. Over the years I have sadly had to attend many other incidents of sudden death in children due to various causes. Not all these events will be recorded in this book as there are too many and they are very distressing. I also detail many other incidents of death within these pages. This book is about the ambulance service and the role of paramedic, so death is common and cannot be avoided. It is however also a book of hope and faith. In chapter 4 you will read about a paediatric death in which I hope to offer some solace, however small, to the reader.

Chapter 2 – Millennium

Pause for thought:
"We will not believe more than we know, and we will not live higher than our beliefs"
-Albert Mohler[1]

For the last ten weeks of 1999 I completed a further 6 weeks of a residential training programme for paramedics at our services training school in Deanshanger, near Milton Keynes Buckinghamshire. Following this I was required to spend 4 weeks working in the operating theatres at Stoke Mandeville hospital where I needed to be observed undertaking 25 intubations and as many cannulation procedures as possible. I would also spend some time in the delivery suite at the maternity unit and in cardiology.

These early days in the ambulance service were great fun and the banter on station was hilarious. Staff spent a lot of time socialising with each other and the camaraderie was strong. We would often have station car washes and raise hundreds of pounds for the social club fund to buy new equipment. Many station discos took place at the Nalgo Club across the road from the ambulance station and after staff would often bundle into the back of the ambulance for a free ride into town to continue boozing.

In those early days in the ambulance service it was often the case that you wouldn't turn a wheel all day, but spend the entire shift on the ambulance station, a luxury that is sadly now long gone. By now I had been in the ambulance service for over two years but had not been to a serious road traffic incident. So, what happened next was a real shock.

We were sent to a car in a field near Dagnall, the police were already on scene and the fire service was en-route. Someone had reported seeing the headlights of a car in a field shining through the trees that ran along the side of the road. It was a summers evening, and just starting to cool as it was getting dark. A police officer had been dispatched to attend the abandoned car report, and after looking over the vehicle noticed a foot sticking out from underneath. The driver had crashed his car, not wearing a seat belt he had been ejected through the open sunroof and his own car had somehow landed on top of him.

We couldn't get to his arm or hand, so I managed to insert a cannula into a vein in his ankle as we waited for the fire service to arrive. There was no response from the patient, and we could not get close to him to put on Oxygen. Once the fire service was on scene, they asked what I needed, and I suggested if the patient had any chance then we needed the car off him as soon as possible. The fire crews literally just picked up the car, and as they did, I felt a moment of hope as his hands seemed to assist in pushing the car upwards, but then his arms just fell away. His hands had been burned by the red-hot exhaust pipe and stuck to its metal. Very sadly the weight of the car had crushed his chest. I believe if he had been wearing a seatbelt, he would have walked away uninjured.

Later that year I attended a hanging, the first of many to come.

It was now January 2002. An incident I had attended just a few months earlier in 2001 had seriously affected me. A young girl aged just 21 had unintentionally taken an insulin overdose. She had wanted to eat some sweets at the cinema and to counter its effect she had given herself some extra insulin. Her mum had spent several hours during that night trying to reverse the hypoglycaemic state she was experiencing by giving her sweet drinks and food. After each brief period of recovery and lucidness she would collapse again into a diabetic coma. Eventually her family called 999.

I arrived on scene expecting to be dealing with a diabetic problem and was directed upstairs to a back bedroom. The person who had greeted us said nothing to cause us any concern, but in fact appeared quite calm. The time we had taken to arrive on scene was over 25 minutes as the location was 17 miles from the ambulance station. I walked into the bedroom to find this young woman in cardiac arrest, and her mother frantically doing chest compressions with the patient still on her bed. We quickly placed her onto the floor which is necessary for effective CPR. We carried out further resuscitation and with just a single dose of IV adrenaline she had a return of spontaneous circulation (known as ROSC). In hospital she was put into an induced coma, but unfortunately, she had sustained irreversible brain damage due to hypoxia before the ambulance had arrived and died a few days later.

What was significant for me at this time was that one of our station managers, paramedic Mark Begley, lived just around the corner from this young lady. If only he had been able to have been contacted in some way maybe a different outcome could have been possible. Several of us at Stoke Station discussed this further over the next few months and subsequently I, Mark Begley, Richard Rolfe and Chris Jackson became the first community responders in Buckinghamshire. We were each supplied with an entire medical kit including a defibrillator, an ambulance service radio in our personal vehicles, drugs and a pager. This was an exciting time for the ambulance service and would in time evolve into the 1000+ dedicated community first responder volunteers (CFR) and co-responders used extensively today by SCAS to support the ambulance service and to serve the local communities. Members include public, military, fire service, police community support officers and coast guard. These volunteers have helped save many lives.

As a paramedic you will be required to support families, relatives and friends as well as patients when they are at the lowest point in their lives. To say that you will encounter people at times of enormous stress, anxiety and fear is an understatement. What you say and do will have a long-lasting effect; people will never forget how you treated their loved one. You will need to be able to stand with people at their darkest times. At times you will be required to deliver the news of death.

Suicide is devastating. This first loss of life I am about to report gave me nightmares. I only saw this once in 23 years and I do not know of any other ambulance person other than my crew mate, who has seen this phenomenon. It is a sad reality that suicide is an all too common call to the ambulance service. When someone has chosen to end their own life, it leaves the family and loved ones devastated and in deep trauma. Anger, fear, blame, guilt, shock, feelings of rejection and abandonment are some of the emotions felt by those who were close to the person. Suicides are always traumatic and upsetting to every ambulance person – without exception.

We were sent to attend a 28-year-old male, believed to be in cardiac arrest. Traffic was heavy and travelling time to scene was nearing 8 minutes. I couldn't help but think to myself en-route that his chances of survival were low. I grabbed every bit of equipment I could carry and rushed into the house towards the downstairs front room. The curtains were drawn, and the room was poorly lit. In front of me was this 28-year-old man, lying on a mattress placed on the floor. I couldn't make sense of his posture!

To this day I can still see his light-coloured red hair. I can still see his contorted face with clenched jaw (trismus). His arms were straight upwards pointing toward the ceiling with his thumbs wrapped between the index and middle fingers (decerebrate posturing), his head was hyper extended and his whole body was off the floor with his feet and shoulders bearing all the weight, like an arched bow. I thought he was having some extremely traumatic seizure, but he was actually in an advanced state of rigor mortis. This abnormal posture is known as Opisthotonos. The cause of his death was from an overdose of a drug called co-proxamol which was withdrawn in 2005 due to its toxicity.

This following event left me stunned; I had not imagined such a reaction. A young man in his early twenties had driven his car deep into thick woodlands where he was sure he would not be discovered, there to end his own life. He carefully ran a hose pipe from the car's exhaust, in through the taped-up window, to allow the toxic fumes to replace the air, and then to wait until he would eventually lose consciousness. He certainly would have succeeded had a jogger who liked to run in the woods, not come across him by chance.

The jogger broke into the car and dragged the limp and lifeless man from the vehicle. On our arrival he was completely flat with a GCS of 3 – deeply unconscious (Glasgow Coma Score). He was suffering the effects of carbon monoxide poisoning and I believe a few more minutes and he would have succeeded in taking his own life. We worked quickly and soon had him on high flow oxygen as his haemoglobin would be saturated with deadly levels carbon monoxide. My crew mate was soon driving as fast as he could safely go, having already made a priority call ahead to the receiving hospital. We got a few miles down the road when he started to regain his consciousness, and then, he literally started screaming, a gut-wrenching agonising scream. My initial thought was he was in severe pain, but I soon realised this wasn't the case; his screams were emotional pain, the pain and shock of still being alive. He then just kept repeating 'why, why, why' over and over. He wanted to be dead and we had stolen that from him. For the first time in my career I came to realise that not everyone wants rescuing, not everyone wants to live in that moment, because something in their life is so terribly painful for them that only dying can seem to stop it.

I know this young man had some issues with his *sexual identity*. I also know he went off to Portsmouth to be treated in a hyperbaric chamber. I do not know how his life continued thereafter but I have always held on to a hope that he somehow found a way to live with his emotional pain.

You are stamped with the image of God:

At stake with suicide is the value of human life. This value God has put on life is of infinite value because you are

11

made in His image, male and female. *You are of infinite value.* In Luke 20 Jesus is challenged when being asked if we should pay taxes to Caesar. Jesus' answer amazes the crowd when asking to see the coin and asking them whose image was on it. Jesus tells them to render unto Caesar what is Caesar's and unto God what is God's. The interesting thing here is that Jesus is saying two things, the coin has Caesar's image so belongs to Caesar therefore give him the taxes, but also you are made in the image of God and are *stamped* in the image of God, which means you belong to God.

When your soul is in agony please turn to God. Turn to God with all your heart and ask Him to give you His Spirit and life. You are a child of God and when we are in pain God draws closer. Consider a child who has fallen over and hurt themselves. When they cry their parent holds them close and intimately whispers in their ear that they are going to be okay – right? Also, when we are hurting, God's love is more intimate and closer and if you listen, you can hear His whispers.

Coming out gay: *The question of homosexuality*

Today many Christians are viewed as prudish who deny pleasure because we live in a grossly hedonistic culture where individual freedom in sexuality reigns. [2]However I would argue that sexuality is central to what makes us human and is found written into our very DNA. I believe humankind was created to be a sexual being by God and that sex is intrinsically good, 'For everything created by God is good' (1 Tim. 4:4). So, as we have looked at a story where someone was so distressed by their sexuality that they tried to end their own life, I would like to try and look at this subject further.

Firstly, in Genesis 2:18 The Lord said, 'It is not good for man to be alone'. Without a female companion man alone could not fully realise his humanity or reproduce. It is clear humankind was created as a sexual being by God. What is more than this is that we have a spiritual dimension to our nature having been made in the image of God as recorded in the creation poem of Genesis 1:27. God created us male and female to foster intimacy and what follows is the divine benediction to procreate (Gen. 1:28). The normal biblical pattern in marriage is frequent sexual intercourse which should be mutually reciprocated between both spouses (1 Cor. 7:2-5). Now I would like to consider what it means to be gay.

A work colleague we will call John had recently announced very publicly via a social networking site that he is gay. In his announcement he expressed his deep agonising and depression over the worry he had gone through regarding what other people were going to think of him. His revelation was unexpected and surprised me. I decided to comment on his timeline, 'good for you mate – be happy'. Reading through other people's comments I felt overwhelmed by the kind regard he was being sent from many friends and work colleagues. I believe it must have been very difficult for him to have taken this step as he is a very shy and introverted person.

Previously, John's mental state had caused me serious concerns. Working for the Ambulance service can be very emotive, and John had been displaying a very depressive and low mood. I and several colleagues raised our concerns with senior management which enabled him to receive the right help. He was supported through several channels including counselling and occupational health, for his depression. It is only now with hindsight that I can see the cause behind his mental health struggles and low mood.

When I was much younger an old friend from school took his own life, aged just 17 years. John's situation had brought this to mind, because as the years have gone by, I have often wondered if his death was linked to his sexuality. Looking back, my school friend had demonstrated an effeminate demeanour. Back then being gay was much more a taboo than it is today.

Christian attitudes towards homosexuality

On reflection there are many interesting issues that require some consideration. Does my comment on the social networking site come into conflict with my Christian position, as some Christian denominations condemn homosexuality as sin? A recent sermon I listened to described only one unpardonable sin. It was the failure to believe in Jesus Christ as the very Son of God and that He purchased a full pardon for our sins on the cross. I am reminded that no one sin needs more grace than another. The rejection of Jesus is the one sin He cannot atone for. If you want to know more about this, please read chapter 13. I am also mindful to love the sinner, not the sin. Jesus throughout his ministry welcomed the sinner and came for the lost not the righteous. It is only when we die that the opportunity to receive Christ is over. Let us be very clear, we are *all* sinners and equally need His grace.

Further reflection has challenged my previously held assumptions as it has become evident that the issue of homosexuality is a hotly debated topic. Many biblical scholars have greatly varying views on what the bible has to say about homosexuality and same sex relationships. Many scholars believe that condemnation in Old Testament scripture was about homosexual rape and prostitution in Pagan temples, not same sex relationships. The New Testament passages such as 1 Corinthians 6:9-11, a so-called proof text, is contentious. The Greek work 'arsenokoitai' which is often translated homosexual offenders in this passage has no exact meaning in modern language, many scholars arguing that it referred to customers who would rent young boys. Paul continues his discourse in verse 11 offering salvation to *all* who come to the Lord.

God works in relationships and no door is ever shut to Him, and no person is outside His grace. Could it be that with no clear definition of this crucial word in Greek (arsenokoitai), that its modern translation reflects society's own prejudices? The next few paragraphs will try to answer this and is quite theological, so if this subject does not interest you then please move on to chapter 3.

[3]Two millennia of Church history have largely demonstrated the condemnation of same-sex practices. For the [4]Church today this subject is a religious and moral issue and one that is very controversial, divisive and hotly debated. [5]Some conservative Christians will immediately judge and condemn homosexual practices based on Christian tradition, biblical interpretation and sexual ethics. [6]Some liberal Christians who support homosexuality see the commitment of a life-long relationship as its moral value. From a Christian standpoint, what position should we take? This article will present more than one point of view in the hope of searching for direction.

[7]At this point it is necessary to understand that in searching for a rule, principle, command or model for an answer to base a point of view on, great caution is necessary as morality and Biblical ethics are a complex issue. Beginning with Leviticus 18 and 20 which are regarded as key biblical verses, the [3]traditionalist view maintains these passages prohibit same sex sexual activity. This prohibition is not only set alongside other commands forbidding bestiality, incest and child sacrifice, but also with other more common and perhaps less immoral illicit sexual activities (Lev. 18: 6ff). [8]Some liberal revisionists argue that the same sex union prohibition described in these Old Testament passages was in the context of homosexual cult prostitution in pagan temples. [7]These biblical commands come from a time and society that was vastly different from ours, [9]therefore seeking to find moral answers from laws that applied to ancient Israelite culture is highly problematic.

[9]Most scholars agree that not all Old Testament laws and codes are binding today but agree that where a stipulation is explicitly renewed in the New Testament it is contemporary. This turns our attention to the material in the New Testament narratives. According to the traditionalists view, in 1

Corinthians 6:9-10 and Timothy 1:9-10 Paul addresses same-sex activity and regards it as serious sin. Similarly, Paul's letter to the Romans (1:18-32) affirms that by rejecting the natural order the pagan in committing same sex sexual acts is rebelling against God[16]. For the revisionist however, such texts are contentious. The exact meaning of the Greek word 'arsenokoitai' often translated as homosexual offenders in these passages is ambiguous. Many scholars argue that Paul's reference was to condemn older men who would rent young boys, thereby rejecting God. [8]It is therefore asserted that Paul did not have consenting same sex activity in mind.

All references to same-sex union in the scriptures are troublesome in that they say very little in their subject material. [7]When seeking to know how people ought to live or not live we are connecting with ethics. Seeking further theological guidance, what can be expressed with greater certainty is God's original purpose and design for sex which is implicit in the natural created order. Some [10]theologians assert that the sexual complementarities of only male and female are the reflection of God's image (Gen. 1:27). It cannot rightly be disputed that the male and female genitalia have intended biological function for procreation, therefore a solid argument may be made that anal intercourse violates the natural design[11].

Direction must follow hope for the homosexual individual seeking monogamous sexual intimacy. We are all living with sexual temptation and share a common humanity and fallen nature. [11]Same-sex attraction for many people is a natural and unquestionable part of their human identity. It is undoubtedly clear that the biblical writers understood same-sex sexual activity as ostensibly wrong[3] and the Church view today remains that homosexual practice falls short of the Christian ideal. We all come to the gospel in our brokenness. We must deal lovingly with people in our church who struggle with their sexual orientation and affirm the person as a child of God, rather than denounce and exclude them. [12]Many homosexual Christians display great agape love and God can use their situation creatively.

Part two

This article has briefly looked at two opposing Christian ethical responses, the frequently expounded traditionalist (Biblicist) view and the familiar liberal Protestant view. According to [13]some, a traditional interpretation could be natural moral law but only in the sense of absolute truth that is grounded in the Christian faith because it is written in our hearts by God. Some theologians assert that fallen humanity has perverted God's natural laws in its heart and must turn to scripture for guidance. That objective reality, they observe, is found in the law of nature, but cannot be perfected. The liberal Christian view may be seen as leaning toward utilitarianism, in that relationships are seen to maximise people's desires and preferences[6]. The moral philosopher [14]Jeremy Bentham's hedonistic outlook took the view that something was right if it created the greatest amount of happiness. For Bentham and the liberal Christian, there is no absolute categorical view and no essential difference between homosexuality and heterosexuality. Both the liberal and conservative Christian equally understand that the bible teaches us that a loving sexual relationship is fulfilling and forms part of our essential being and sense of worth. The differences lay in our hermeneutics and ethical position.

The final approach to ethics I used in this article leans towards Christian situation ethics, without having lost sight of the sinful nature at work in *all* people and recognising our need for grace (Tit. 2:11). While the church has pointed out that same-sex union was not the original purpose of God's created order for procreation, it does express the infinite value of every individual (Gen. 1:27). Situational ethics asserts the concept of unconditional agape (selfless) love, judging the rightness of the action in relation to its situation. [15]It recognises the individual's authentic humanity and emphasises the supremacy of love. Situation ethics is a consequential theory in that the primary action of love is the outcome. This

17

may be considered an authentic approach to Christian ethics because it is based on Jesus' teachings; love God and love your neighbour (Mk 12:30-31).

Chapter 3 Choking, 'Heimlich Manoeuvre' (ROSC a thump and a knock on the head)

Pause for thought. Is it possible to bring someone back from the dead?

At a cardiac arrest of a 23-year-old male, the father's only words that were spoken were "please save my son", he was in utter shock. Even as I write this many years later, I feel a lump in my throat. My reply came back through a slightly cracking voice "we will do everything we can sir". This event is testimony to bystander CPR (in this case by his brother) and a single determination not to give up, to give 100% of yourself and a willingness to resuscitate someone even when the odds seemed stacked against success. If you do this as a paramedic or any other helper, you will always go home, even if it is with a heavy heart, with a clear conscience that you did everything in your power to save that person's life. I don't care how brilliant you are, if you are not prepared to give someone 100% you should not be a health care professional. They deserve it, it is their right, and you would not expect anything less in the care of your own family members.

This 23-year-old man had, 30 minutes earlier, complained to his family of a sudden back ache and taken himself to his bed. I asked the brother who found him collapsed, if he had indicated whether the pain was in his upper back, as I suspected a cardiac cause, but he said he didn't know. This patient was now completely lifeless on the bedroom floor, ashen grey and clammy. His dilated pupils stared emptily, without focus as though what had animated his life was no longer behind them. One minute there was life, but in this moment he was dead.

We hurriedly began to prepare equipment for advanced life support and charge the defibrillator, while his brother continued to deliver good chest compressions. Between me, my crewmate Serg Fontenla, who is a talented paramedic, and

Simon Lukas, a very skilled and experienced paramedic team leader, we delivered a staggering 15 shocks, each one jolting his limp body and causing his arms to spasmodically jerk. Initially it all seemed futile, he would have a momentary return of cardiac output only to re-arrest again and again, each passing moment seemingly more desperate. Eventually there came a faint pulse and his colour slowly started to improve. It would be many minutes before it would be safe to move him, once in a slightly more stable condition. On arrival at hospital he went straight into the 'cath' lab for PPCI but arrested a further 2 more times during the procedure and was again defibrillated. A major coronary artery was completely occluded, and he had suffered a massive heart attack. Later that evening this young man went off to the Hammersmith Hospital on ECMO. He later began a journey to recovery but with continuing medical support. He will likely require a heart transplant for any future quality of life. Most importantly, he lived.

Choking at Pub

It was just after 1:00pm and we were sitting in Aylesbury town Market Square on roadside standby, at a time when crews we far less busy than they are today (2004). As usual, we were passing the time with chit chat. My crew mate Big D (Dave Dunlop) would then suddenly break out into an Elvis Presley song; he knew every lyric to every song and even had the Elvis lip curl thing going on - not a pretty sight I can tell you. As often was the case, many shifts were routine and nothing too challenging would happen. It could be like this for a couple of months. I wouldn't say you become complacent or aren't ready for the unexpected, but it would be unhealthy to be in a constant state of high alert or to worry about what might happen next. Then you get that job and it sounds serious, and usually you would have a gut feeling that would tell you this is as it has been reported, this is going to be real.

We are told a female had choked on her meal in a restaurant and was now unconscious, possibly in cardiac arrest. We were also told there was no bystander CPR in progress. The incident was less than a mile away and did not give us a great deal of time to make any formulated plan or to prepare. We raced to the scene discussing in this short amount of time what equipment we would take in with us and who will do what. On arrival as we entered the restaurant, we could see on the floor a lifeless woman, lying on her back, with no signs of life. No one has attempted to help her, and she has no respiratory effort. As an attendant at such jobs, you start to feel your own heart racing as adrenaline courses through your veins. The people around this lady carried on eating their meals and as we rushed over to help, they seemed to be oblivious to what was happening and the whole scenario seemed surreal.

At this time paramedics carried their own orange paramedic box containing their own advanced airway adjuncts and drugs. We first attempted back slaps and then abdominal thrusts, previously known as the Heimlich manoeuvre, but this had not effected any change. She had a pulse of 123 beats per minute, but her airway remained totally occluded and time was against her. If we couldn't remove whatever was in her airway, she was going to die and very quickly. Big D got the defibrillator and oxygen ready as I prepared my laryngoscope and Magill's forceps taken from my kit. This equipment would help me inspect the patient's airway and laryngopharynx to the back of the throat. And there I could see it, a large piece of grisly meat below her epiglottis. On the second attempt I managed to remove it and in an act of loathing for this piece of meat flicked it away. It was then the guy still sitting eating his meal next to us exclaimed 'flipping heck' or words to that effect. I then intubated this lady and assisted her breathing for her until she arrived at the resuscitation room. On arrival she had begun to make increased attempts to breath for herself.

Following this we attended another incident and on our return to hospital we checked in on our lady. She was now extubated and was sitting up but was agitated and confused, no doubt caused by her ordeal and a lack of oxygen. The following day we went up to the ward to check on her once gain and this time she was sitting in bed, eating a much softer meal and had completely recovered. We chatted to her and I don't believe she really knew how lucky she was to be alive, but we were buzzing with joy.

This is how 'Big D' describes the same incident   *'Did you say' Heimlich Manoeuvre'?*

Big D is an old hand paramedic with a predisposition to tell 'tall tales' and here recounts how we saved the life of this choking woman (for fun)! He recalled: "We was called to a restaurant" he would begin, "to a distressed choking woman. Following the choking algorithm, I asked her to try and cough, but she was unable. I then proceeded to administer 5 back slaps but with no success. I knew things had become desperate and I would have to escalate my life saving skills even further. It was a real emergency, so I lifted her dress, pulled her knickers down and applied a big wet sloppy lick to her left buttock with my slippery wet tongue. The woman was so shocked and outraged that she violently convulsed and the piece of meat shot out her mouth and across the floor. Yep I said, that's how you do the *Hind Lick Manoeuvre*" (Big D)

My crew mate Chris, known affectionately as 'Simbo' and I were asked to attend an address of a male patient. Details were a little sketchy and I can't fully remember what we were told, but I do remember there was no information given requiring us to wait for the police. We entered the property which reeked of cigarette smoke, and sitting in his armchair was our patient, a man we shall call Jimmy although this isn't his real name. Jimmy was rolling a cigarette and lit it up, all the while nonchalant to the fact that two ambulance men were standing in his lounge asking him questions. He just blanked us.

After several minutes of further enquiry as to the reasons why Jimmy might have called us, two police officers suddenly walked into the room surprised by the fact that we were there at all. They then informed us that they had requested ambulance attendance but with a warning - Jimmy was known to pull out knives on ambulance crews. Our ambulance control had been told that we should not approach the property until the police were on scene. True to his form, as this information was disclosed Jimmy pulled out a knife and was promptly bent up by the two police officers and taken into custody. It wouldn't be long before we encountered Jimmy again.

A couple of weeks passed, and I was again crewed with Simbo on a day shift. We came off a roundabout onto Exchange Street in Aylesbury and was a little confused when we saw another ambulance parked up, with blue lights flashing and what appeared to be a man half under the ambulance with an oxygen mask on. The driver Mark C. was almost in tears pacing frantically and declaring, "I've killed him, I've killed him". What on earth had gone on here, had they run this man over? We got the answers from Deneen Shaw who had been in the back of the ambulance, conveying our recent acquaintance Jimmy to hospital. Jimmy had decided to unbuckle his seat belt, get up and try to strangle Deneen, naturally she screamed out for help. Mark pulled over, ran from the cab and quickly ejected Jimmy out of the side door of the ambulance but he landed on his head and was knocked out. Fortunately, Jimmy had no lasting injury. Simbo and I conveyed Jimmy to hospital for observation; no complaint was sought from either party.

Witnessed arrest:

We were called to attend a man in his seventies who was acutely unwell. As was often the case, this man had no chest pain but one look at him told you he was having a myocardial infarct or MI for short, commonly known as a heart attack. He was ashen grey and clammy and looked frightened.

We rapidly attached the ECG dots to his chest after drying him a little with a towel and continued to offer reassurance as we attended to him. In the room were his wife, daughter and a granddaughter of about ten year of age. Suddenly his eyes rolled back, and he let out a deep guttural groan as he slumped in the armchair. Displayed on our monitor was ventricular fibrillation in all 12 leads; he was now in cardiac arrest. The daughter rushed the family out of the room, realising what was happening.

I rapidly pulled off the monitoring leads and as I did so my crew mate Big D gave him a precordial thump, a sharp thump to the sternum used in a witnessed VF cardiac arrest to restart the heart. Well, I think it would be fair to say it was a good gyaku-zuki, a karate style punch from the hip. Dave's basic karate skills had failed though, so we placed him on the floor and managed to put in a shock from the defibrillator. Within a few moments this patient was alert and talking, seemingly unaware of what had just taken place but a little confused as to why he was now on the floor with a 'sore' chest. Dave and I received the most heart-warming thank you from his family and following treatment in hospital he made a complete recovery.

Cardiac arrest in a public place:

Dylan Robson and I were dispatched to Westcott community centre to a male patient. At first, we were told we were attending a collapse, with no further details. This was in the days before satellite navigation and computer aided dispatch screens, and as was often the case an update would come via the radio Comms and would often mean things had worsened for the patient. About six miles into the journey we were told the call was being upgraded to a cardiac arrest, with bystander CPR in progress.

We thought it would be wise ask control for a second crew to back us up, only to be told that none were available, so we asked for support from a solo car responder. On arrival we rushed our equipment into the corridor where the patient's son was continuing chest compressions on his father. The patient was quite a big man, lying on his back his stomach was some size and an estimate of his weight would have been well in excess of 24 stone. We were told by his son that his dad had recently been discharged from ITU. Everything was going well at this point with our resuscitation efforts. Derek had arrived on scene as our back up on a response car, so we had enough hands to move this heavy man onto the stretcher. With help from the son we lifted the stretcher and pulled the lever to allow the legs to drop down into position.

The stretcher came crashing down heavily hitting the floor from a height of about 4'0". The legs had been locked firmly in place so what had just happened? When we looked a little closer it was evident that the metal frame had sheared in two. These stretchers were designed to take weights in excess of 40 stone, and this had never happened before. We continued our efforts with resuscitation but were still unable to get another ambulance for backup. Our next move was to try and load the stretcher onto the sliding platform on the ambulance while still carrying on the CPR, but we were unable to secure the stretcher because of the twisted metal frame. We considered if we could transport this man on the floor, but this was unsafe in the least and was not an option. By now we had been doing advanced life support in excess of 45 minutes and the patient had been in cardiac arrest for about an hour. The son pleaded with us to stop.

Collectively we all agreed that to continue was not an option and doing so was causing great distress to the son. The decision to stop resuscitation was agreed. At this time, the ambulance service policy was clear that resuscitation was always to be continued in a public place unless the person was in a state of rigor mortis, decomposition or with injuries incompatible with life such as hemicorporectomy. A witnessed arrest as this was, must be resuscitated to hospital, stopping was outside protocol and very unusual.

Because we now had a body, the hospital would not receive this person into their care. This meant we were required to transport him to the local mortuary. Again, this was outside normal protocol and something that had never happened before in my career. It took several hours to book him in and complete all the legalities required. The following day I was asked by a senior manager to give a valid reason for stopping CPR. My answer was rescuer exhaustion and that is where the matter was concluded as this was a valid reason to stop.

Chapter 4 Death Experience

Pause for thought: Is death the final word or a gateway to eternal life?

A crew and a rapid response car were dispatched to attend a man in his fifty's named Danny, his wife Mary had called the ambulance because he had collapsed moments earlier. On arrival Danny was sitting on the front doorstep, ashen grey and soaked with sweat, clutching his chest. He looked very unwell; the crew knew this man was having a massive heart attack and were already deeply concerned. Mary then announces, "do you know Shane, he's our nephew and works as a paramedic?"

The crews looked at each other, and under their breath muttered a few words of concern, often referred to as expletives. Their worst fear was then realised a few moments later when my uncle Danny went into cardiac arrest. The crews worked frantically together, now feeling the added pressure and stress of working to resuscitate Danny in the knowledge that he was the relative of a colleague and friend. They defibrillated Uncle Danny in-between rounds of CPR and got a weak pulse, but he then immediately re-arrested for the second time with no signs of life. As each minute raced by his chances of survival seemed to be slipping away. Once on the stretcher in the back of the ambulance another round of intravenous drugs were given, with further CPR and another set of shocks. This time they had some success, they found another weak pulse. The ECG confirmed a massive coronary event and he was rushed to hospital.

Pause for thought: You are of infinite value.

My Uncle Danny was later transferred to High Wycombe hospital and then onto the Hammersmith hospital in London where he had a coronary artery by-pass graft and made a full recovery. Thank you so much to Vince Burden, 'Big' Daz Tompkins and Michelle B, you saved the life of a deeply loved Uncle who is also a father, husband, grandfather and the brother of my own dad. I know how much this put you all on a high afterward; it's in such moments where we know beyond any doubt that a life has been saved, and that's why we work in such emotive situations. A thank you seems inadequate when you save any life, which has infinite value.

A few months later, my dad and I went to see my Uncle, who was now home and recovering well. He wanted to discuss with me something that had really puzzled him. We sat around his kitchen table; Auntie Mary had made a pot of hot tea and then sat with us while we chatted. My Uncle then asked me if I knew the cardiac rehab nurse Rob and wanted to know why he had asked him if he had any kind of experiences when he had died. Uncle Danny then recounted what had happened in his experience when he had suffered a cardiac arrest. He told us that he had watched the whole thing from a distance as the crew worked on him, following them from about 20 feet away as they pushed the stretcher along the long footpath and onto the back of the ambulance. I told my uncle I would ask Rob when I got a chance as I did know him well.

It is recorded in the bible that the apostle Paul experienced what might be described as an 'out of body' experience. Paul wrote in 2 Corinthians 12:1-2, "*I must go on boasting. Although there is nothing to be gained, I will go on to visions and revelations from the Lord. I know a man in Christ who was caught up to the third heaven. Whether it was in the body or out of the body I do not know – God knows*".

Scholars agree that Paul was talking about himself here in the third person. An out of body or near-death experience in the Christian life is an unexplained phenomenon. Although my Uncle Danny's experience is not uncommon and makes a good story here, it leaves a lot unanswered. Searching for a mystical truth is warned against in the bible along with any type of occult practice. If we try and enter the spirit realm ourselves, we may allow legal rights to demonic influence. If we want the truth about God and the spirit realm the answers we seek are found in the scriptures of the bible. If you want a tangible experience of God then come to know Christ Jesus through worship, draw close to Him and He will draw close to you. In this way you may know God through the Holy Spirit. You can have a personal relationship with the creator of the universe!

Some months later after speaking with my Uncle Danny, I was walking through the A&E department and I bumped into Nurse Rob as he was passing. I asked him about this and he told me that he was collating people's experiences for research and that over many years working on a cardiac ward where successful resuscitation was common, he had heard hundreds on similar stories and this kind of experience was very common. For me as a paramedic, this is the only time I have heard this kind of story regarding my job. I am not sure what any of this means and am only reporting it because I believe that what my uncle had experienced was completely real to him. However, below I am going to write about another experience which is a real event that is highly emotive and difficult to fully understand.

I would like to warn the reader, reading this will be distressing and involves a baby. It is not recounted for sensationalism but has a very important underlying message. If you are easily distressed please pass this next part by. For anyone who has ever lost a chid I truly hope there is a glimmer of comfort found here. This book is about the role of a paramedic. It is also about God and a Christian point of view. This event is true in every detail.

On this shift I had no crew mate and no car was available for me to work on, so I put all my things onto a regular ambulance vehicle which I would man on my own. Some of the shift had passed and I had just finished my meal break. The 'red phone' in the crew room rang and I was told I would be backing up Tracy Mould who was on a car with a sick baby, asking for immediate backup. The baby was a neonate, being just 7 days old. These incidents are always the toughest to cope with and cause great emotional conflict with all involved. Most paramedics feel a lack of control and desperation in these distressing situations and are filled with dread.

As I pulled up at the address Tracy came running out with a lifeless baby in her arms, her immediate gut response wanting to go immediately to hospital. The baby was mottled and ashen and his appearance looked close to death, although he was still breathing (moribund). We both agreed the correct approach was to carry out proper ventilation and cardiac support. At hospital, a team of paediatric doctors were ready to receive the baby.

I remember feeling deep sorrow as the team looked after him. He was placed in an incubator and was in a deep coma, being mechanically ventilated and anaesthetised. I think looking back that the situation had seriously challenged my deepest held beliefs, how can a good God allow such things to happen? As I stood there looking on, I prayed from a place within me that I have rarely prayed from before. It was a heartfelt prayer from the innermost core of my being, "God, I don't understand, but if you are somehow in this, if you have all things under your sovereign control, please show me that you are in this situation, as awful as it is, God make him move his arms now". The baby boy, who was totally sedated and comatose, moved both of his arms as I looked at him, no one was touching him, his arms moved away from his body.

The baby was later transferred to Great Ormond Street hospital and sadly died the following day. I don't have the answers as to why; I don't think any answer is adequate or could ever be. I can't tell any parent that they will ever stop feeling deep pain and sorrow at such a terrible loss. The loss of any child is the saddest most heart-breaking experience a person can have. Nothing can make the pain go away. The only thing I can see is hope. This hope, for the Christian, is that children, lacking accountability, die and go to heaven. This is the Christian view (2 Samuel 12:23). You may not hold onto a faith and believe such a statement to be true. If you have lost a child, he or she will be in heaven with God right now regardless of what *you* believe because God receives those who haven't rejected Him. My prayer is that you will not reject His gift of eternal life for yourself. Please believe this. Please see chapter 13.

Pause for thought: Religion is man's attempt to cover his sin by his own works

My Testimony

I joined the Ambulance service back in 1998 and at that time was a martial arts fanatic, also spending many years pursuing 'a spiritual path' which had included mysticism and occult practices. I believed I was trying to establish a relationship with the Divine by my own merit and effort. In truth, I was in bondage to these practices and filled with anger and a feeling of emptiness. It seriously impacted my relationship with my wife.

After meeting a Christian and Spirit filled man at work, through prayer things began to change. This person seemed to embody all that I had been searching for. Both he and his wife demonstrated the love of God as they both walked the Christian path. They both were living a life in a *personal* relationship with Jesus.

What happened next was truly profound. I woke up one morning as I had done for several years to begin my day with esoteric meditation but knew at that moment, I would never do any of these mystic practices again. I was instantly set free, experiencing a new joy and happiness, I have never looked back. I realised I couldn't merit my own way to God or trust my own goodness. It was by His grace alone. Are you meditating regularly? I would like you to consider this question, yes you may feel some relaxation, but do you experience real joy in your life? Are you spending countless hours trying to save yourself (mukti or samsara) – you just can't do it. Jesus has already paid for your redemption and offers you His free gift of eternal life. It is that simple. You can't earn what only God can give. You are not guaranteed a tomorrow.

Going forward life continues to deliver many hard knocks; suffering is a guaranteed part of the human spectrum of experience. But I know that Jesus walks this path with me. I would rather have his companionship than walk life's path alone. God sees you as someone who He wants to have a relationship with Him.

Chapter 5 Right to Die – *'Allowing a natural death'*

On this shift I was crewed with my permanent crew mate and friend Steve Davis (not the snooker player for those of you who are old enough to remember). The following event happened at a time when as a rule it wasn't common practice to have an advance care directive or living will in place and this lady hadn't made one either. In fact, we had only been asked to attend by her GP to carry out a 12 lead ECG for the community nurse who was on scene, but this put us in a difficult ethical position.

We were informed that this 87-year-old female who we will call Ms. A, was presenting with severe shortness of breath. On arrival I was greeted by the community nurse who informed me that Ms. A would vehemently refuse to go to hospital. After introducing myself to this frail elderly lady I asked her permission to take some basic observations, which she agreed to. It was clear from her presentation that she was very ill.

From further clinical assessment of Ms. A, it was evident from a medical position that she was desperately ill and would benefit from immediate hospital care. Ms. A's wishes were very different from the standard we expect as health care providers. It was her resolute wish to remain at home even to the point of dying. Having discussed with Ms. A her options she was able to clearly demonstrate her understanding of all the information I had given her, she understood what her treatment options were and had clearly demonstrated her decision at that time. This assessment of her demonstrated she had mental capacity in relation to the issue of refusing to travel to a hospital.

As a health care provider, I have a legal obligation as a 'duty of care' to provide a reasonable standard of care. I am also aware of ethical implications surrounding a patient's right to receive of refuse treatment. Being registered with the

Health Care and Professions Council paramedics have a legal responsibility to adhere to their [2]Standards of Conduct, Performance and Ethics.

The caring side of me wanted to treat Ms. A thereby promoting her physical well-being, taking her to hospital where my role as an ambulance paramedic would have been seen to have been fulfilled. However, I recognised that Ms. A had every right to refuse to travel to hospital and I felt that it was her sincere wish to die at home. Ms. A's son did not support his mother's wishes and insisted that we take her to hospital against her will and forcibly in necessary. His views were different from his sisters who wanted her mother's wishes to be honoured. It is also illegal to force someone into hospital who is demonstrating capacity, and has refused. This would be kidnap.

It is evident from the account given in this story that certain ethical questions were raised. Attention will be drawn to the following questions:

- Is it intrinsically wrong to fail to prolong life for as long as possible and at any cost?
- Is allowing someone to die naturally, without medical intervention, morally wrong?
- Is this a form of passive euthanasia?
- Is it wrong to resuscitate someone against their express wishes when they clearly can demonstrate the mental capacity to refuse treatment?
- Are we effectively allowing suicide by not enforcing treatment?
- Whose choice is it anyway?
- What should be my Christian response as a medic regarding this matter?

Pause for thought:

You cannot get into death except by life: You cannot get into the next life except by death.

As a Christian I believe that we are accountable before God for our lives (Rom. 14:12) and this includes looking after our physical health (1 Cor. 6:12-20). However, should physical death be resisted at any cost, when for the Christian being absent from this body is to be with the Lord (2 Cor. 5:1-8)? There is no given Christian defence or acceptable reason for prolonging life without any constraints. This is not to say that we should pursue death but recognise that it is an inevitable appointment ordained by God (Heb. 9:27-28). A question that must be asked in this event is who should choose and what are the consequences?

To deny someone choice is to deny them autonomy and free will. Regarding a competent patient, the right to refuse life-sustaining treatment has been given precedence to the patient above that of the clinician or anyone else[3]. Ms A's choices, however, would impact her son and challenge my own ethics. This autonomy-based approach is in some sense virtue ethics, in the sense that by using reason, the individual intension becomes an act of the human will. Virtue ethics also considers what it is to be fully human and examines a qualitative dimension to life[4], which is now missing through illness. It might be argued that the flourishing of life, what Aristotle called *Eudemonia,* is now unattainable as death approaches. From a theological perspective, depending on one's religious conviction, the Christian ethical virtue of hope may or may not be expressed or experienced by the patient (1 Cor. 12:27-13:13).

Allowing Ms. A to die naturally is unequivocally not a form of passive euthanasia because there is no bringing about a death due to the deliberate inaction of others[5]. Autonomy to forgo life-preserving treatment is not suicide when there is a lethal disease already present and no self-inflicted injury occurs[6]. Therefore, respecting a patient's self determination to decline medical intervention, when curative treatment is no longer possible, honours human dignity[7].

Clearly Ms. A's health and wellbeing were the central concern of all those who were caring for her, medical staff and family members included. It became apparent to me during this time and also later on that each person's ideals and concept of 'health and wellbeing' were different depending on each person's perspective, social conditioning, beliefs and relationship to the patient, not excluding the patient herself. The same set of characteristics of each person was also the driving factors that seemed to shape their views on death, dying and bereavement. Bearing this in mind, I decided to reflect upon these different perspectives to try and gain a deeper understanding of the events we were all trying to cope with.

[8]Health is defined as being 'a state of complete physical, mental, and social well-being and not merely the absence of disease or infirmity'. This statement declares that the mental and social dimensions to our health are essential for complete well-being and that in their absence we do not have complete health.

From my perspective, my relationship with Ms. A was probably going to be the least in duration and as such would remain mostly impersonal. The clinical side of me wanted to treat the patient promoting her physical well-being at that time and take her to hospital were my role as an ambulance paramedic would have been seen to have been fulfilled. However, I felt that Ms. A had every right to refuse to travel to hospital and I felt completely comfortable with the fact that it was her wish to die at home. I feel that with the right care and under the right circumstances it is better for someone to die in their own familiar environment. The normal processes we expect to encounter within our role as ambulance personnel had been changed. This lady was not asking for my help in the normal sense but needed a strategy that met her wishes. The emphasis was now to provide the best quality of life and end of life care for Ms. A placing her at the heart of the decision process and providing her and the family with all the available help and supporting their psychological care throughout.

Generally, the response of the ambulance service is usually to attend a crisis of some description and the duration we spent with our patients is often less than 1-2 hours. Because the duration of care we provide to the terminally ill is so short I thought it would benefit my practice to look at these different stages of grieving, thereby gaining a deeper understanding of the psychological aspects on death and dying. In 1968 Elizabeth Kubler–Ross[9] introduced a 5-stage theory which recognized that both patients and family may experience these processes, which I have outlined here:

- Denial – The first response is often "No, not me". The patient or family member may seek other opinions or simply ignore what they have been told.
- Anger - This anger is the anger of the dying person towards all the people who continue to live. It is the "Why me" phase and the dying person will reject family effort to help console them.
- Bargaining – This stage the feeling is "Yes me, but....." At this stage, the sick person admits they are probably dying but tries to bargain for extension of their life, these bargains are often made in secret with God or spiritual figures etc.
- Depression – This stage involves preparing for death. It often involves saying goodbye to everyone a person has known and loved. It may involve putting all our affairs in order.
- Acceptance – The dying person adopts a "Yes, it is my time" and is ready to die (during this time friends and relatives need the greatest help).

It should be noted that in addition to this 5-stage theory is it often overlooked that hope will persist throughout all these stages. Kubler-Ross also stated that most people she observed feared dying even more than death itself. The 5 stages, although presented here in a linear fashion, were not meant to be exact periods of time which would replace each other but were considered to exist next to each other and to overlap at times. Also, it has been acknowledged that not all individuals experience all five stages. The theory was an effort to crudely categorise the many experiences patients have when suddenly faced with their own finality. It should be noted that this is only a theory and that no evidence has been presented that people move from stage one through to stage five. We should remember that each person will react in their own individual way. To be effective care providers we need to listen actively to those who are coping with dying.

Our patient, Ms. A, seemed to be totally acceptant of the fact that she was going to die to the point that going to hospital was not an option for her. It seemed like she had skipped all the previous 4 stages of grief and was already at the acceptance stage "Yes, it is my time". Could it have been that she was in the first stage of denial? I don't believe this to be the case because she clearly recognised how unwell she was, and she had also demonstrated her dying wishes. I wondered how much time this elderly lady had spent reflecting on her own mortality in respect of her age and if this had had any bearing on her acceptance of dying. Where was the 'Hope' we are said to have even unto death. Was Ms. A still going to experience some or all the other processes such as anger and depression? I believe she may have although to what extent cannot be stated. Some weeks later I met the community nurse who had first called us to Ms. A and she informed me that this lady had passed away, some 2 weeks after our first contact with her and that in the last few days of her life she had voluntarily gone into a hospice to die.

During the time in which Ms. A had spent in her own home it was necessary to involve other health professions and domiciliary care services which included intermediate care, nursing staff, palliative care providers, social services, liaison with her GP, and the provision of home oxygen, commode and the provision of a bed down stairs. These plans were started at the point when we had all agreed that Ms. A was resolute about dying at home. The family were also involved in the decision process and the Nurse Practitioner who was now involved was going to oversee the finer details.

Biblical ethics affirms the goodness of life in this world and the importance of the viability of all members of society[10]. The Christian and Biblical view of the sanctity of human life is clearly demonstrated in scripture, in that human life is created in the image of God (Gen 9:5-6; Pss. 8:3-5 & 139:3ff; Acts 17:25) and the bible mandates the preservation of life[11]. The Christian may also regard medical care as a gift from God and part of His common grace to humanity[12]. So, should physical death be resisted at any cost? The answer is that there is no Christian defence or acceptable reason for prolonging life without restraint [13]. This is not to say that we should pursue death but recognise that it is an inevitable appointment ordained by God (Heb. 9:29-28). Death is humankind's final earthly experience and a part of life.

Chapter 6 Dying, the Hospice and Healings

Dying well and the Hospice

Pause for thought: 'Death has lost its grip on me

Most people say they would prefer to die at home, yet the reality is that most deaths, a staggering 58 per cent, occur in NHS hospitals. Only 18 per cent happen at home, 17 per cent in care homes, 4 per cent in hospices and 3 per cent elsewhere[2]. These statistics represent modern society and I personally find them disturbing as clearly what most people would prefer and what is happening is very different.

The nineteenth century saw a time of great hospital building. However, the medical profession at that time saw approaching death as a medical failure. Those dying were no longer welcome in hospital and this led to charities funding the creation of special institutions, some of which were called hospices. History had shown that when dying, people often experienced social isolation and loneliness and this became a strong motivation for the development of palliative care and death education in the 1960's, launching the modern hospice as we know it today. Today the modern hospice provides a sanctuary for those nearing death.

[3]Jeanne Garnier, a young widow and bereaved mother established one such institution in Lyon, France, in 1842. To this day there still exists a palliative care service directly from her work. In 1879 an order known as the Sisters of Charity helped change their convent in Ireland to become Our Lady's Hospice for the dying. In the United States, Rose Hawthorne formed an order known as the Dominican Sisters of Hawthorne who established St. Rose's Hospice in Lower Manhattan. Their achievements created some of the preconditions for the modern hospice and palliative care

development. By the mid-twentieth century more emphasis was on cure and rehabilitation in hospitals and dying in hospital had become the norm. At this time, it was usual for doctors to have nothing more to do with those who were dying, and their care was left to the nurses and relatives. This meant that there was less professional interest in caring for those at the end of their lives. This often led to medical neglect. It was this medical neglect that brought about change for the care of those at the end of their life here in Great Britain.

A new view of dying began to emerge which focused on dying with dignity and meaning. An active role developed in caring for the dying. [4]The first 'modern' hospice is said to have been developed in St. Joseph's Hospital in Hackney, East London by Cicely Saunders and established at St. Christopher's Hospice in South London in 1967. Saunders recognized the social, emotional and spiritual aspects of suffering. She believed that pain should be prevented rather than alleviated once it had become established. The hospice's key principles were excellent clinical care, education and research. This was to set the standard for all in this new field of care and became the stimulus for hospice development around the world [4](Saunders 1964). By the mid-1980s there had developed more than 100 hospices around the UK which were also supported by home-support services and the first hospital palliative care teams. We are now moving into a time where Hospice care and Palliative care share a common purpose and are often one model of care which is available to more people regardless of diagnosis, stage of disease or social class.

It is fair to say that some people's deaths are better than others; there are good deaths and bad deaths. Some people die suddenly, previously they seemed in good health and die quickly without any apparent suffering. For others there may be long months of pain and ill health and death is preferred to continued existence. The way in which someone dies then, can have a significant impact not only on the individual but

41

also the loved ones who are left behind, the survivors-to-be/bereaved. The quality of death can affect the quality of grief. Grief associated with bereavement is one of the most profound of all human emotions. When someone close to us dies it is felt as a personal loss and we experience extreme sadness and even depression.

Certain types of bereavement render people especially vulnerable:

- sudden and unexpected death, particularly in tragic circumstances;
- the loss of a child, irrespective of age;
- the loss of a parent during one's childhood;
- several bereavements within a short period of time;
- where the death follows a long or harrowing illness;
- the loss of someone relied upon for emotional or practical support;
- following a history of depression or other mental health problems;
- where the bereaved person lacks family or social networks;
- in circumstances such as disability, poverty or physical ill-health.

According to Bowlby and Parkes the bereavement process may be divided into four phases:

1. Shock and Numbness: During this initial phase, survivors have difficulty processing the information of the loss; they are stunned and numb[5].

2. Yearning and Searching: In this phase, there is a combination of intense separation anxiety and disregard or denial of the reality of the loss. This engenders a desire to search for and recover the lost person. Failure of this search leads to repeated frustration and disappointment[5]

3. Disorganisation and Despair: Individuals often report being depressed, and have difficulty planning future activities. These individuals are easily distracted and have difficulty concentrating and focusing[6]

4. Reorganization: This phase overlaps to some degree with the third phase[6]

Having said this, grief does not have a specific timetable. Each person grieves differently and in their own time.

Stories from two Care Home Residents, as reported by Emily:

First story:

There was this lovely frail lady in her 80's adored by everyone who was called Doris. Doris came to us for care and support on our residential floor at a local Care Home I work at. She held a strong Christian faith and could often be heard singing her favourite song 'Amazing Grace' to the other residents. Doris loved listening to those old hymns and gospel classics.

As Doris's health deteriorated, she unfortunately was put on end of life care and spent her last few weeks in bed. Another carer and I were attending to Doris and making her comfortable, which for me was always special. Whilst we were doing this, she said "my mum is sat over there". Although Doris was end of life care she still had her normal faculties. I asked where her mum was and what was she doing. Doris replied, "she's sat in my armchair smiling at me". Whilst saying this, Doris was very much at peace and seemed so content. Within a week she had passed away. Death is a natural part of human life.

Pause for thought: If it is true that the value of something is measured by what someone else will pay – what is our worth to Him?

Second story:

There was a local man called Peter who came to us from a small village not far from our care home. He was a very quiet and kind man. Peter was previously widowed after losing his wife suddenly. Like Doris he had come to us for support with his physical needs and personal care. Peter never really said much but whenever you saw him, he was happy and smiling. As his health declined Peter would tell me frequently, often when he would get into bed at night, that he could see his wife in his room. He would say she would sit on the end of his bed making sure he was okay, watching over him. Do family come to us to prepare us and tell us it is time to go home? How wonderful this was for him. Peter passed away peacefully in his armchair in his sleep.
      Emily Turvey

Sally's sister Jo (Joanne) was sadly diagnosed with ovarian cancer and her health declined very rapidly. As sisters they were really close to each other. Sally spent some special moments with Jo as her health deteriorated during this time, but they had some beautiful conversations. Sally told me this short story and has given me permission to re-tell it here.
      Jo believed in the continuation of the soul after death and this brought her comfort. As they discussed this together Sally said to Jo to send her a message or sign and to let her know that she was safe when she got to heaven and told her their dad would be waiting for her there. Their dad loved bumble bees, and this was a fond memory they also shared.
      Jo died on the Sunday that week. The following day Sally was booked in to give a donation of blood and wanted to

continue to do so, even though she felt shattered by her loss. It was a comfort that they had both shared the same blood type and Sally could imagine herself helping someone like Jo by giving her donated blood for them.

At the clinic, the nurse seemed friendly and made polite conversation, asking Sally what her middle name was. As Sally now joked, most Sallies are either Sally-Anne as she was, or Sally-Louise. She asked the nurse why she had asked, and the reply was her daughter was also called Sally. The nurse then disappeared for a few minutes before returning. When she came back Sally asked her what her daughter's full name was, and she said she was a Sally-Joanne, known as Sally-Jo. How unusual Sally thought to herself. It was then that a bumble bee gently came by, settled next to Sally as if to say hi, and flew off again.

Sally Anne Taylor

Do you believe in the miraculous? Some true stories are hard to believe especially when it hasn't been your own personal experience. Of course, some people see the miraculous in everyday things such as a flower blossoming or in the birth of a child; these are miracles. But other miracles defy what we know as being in the realm of science, they are just hard to imagine or understand. My own experiences as a Christian have included seeing miracles when people have been healed, right in front of my eyes. I watched in amazement and awe of God as a young woman from my church with advanced scoliosis was healed, her spine just straightened out in front of all who watched. As hands were laid upon her and prayers was offered, the muscles surrounding her back could be seen twitching and through her blouse we saw the movement from curvature to straight take place. She cried with joy.

I would like to mention that not everyone gets healed and this is a mystery. I have seen desperate mothers receive prayer but go on to lose their unborn baby due to a congenital defect. Other people with cancer have sadly died, with no healing taking place at all. God doesn't heal everyone all of the time. But sometimes something happens, and it is supernatural. I would like to tell you about a miracle that goes beyond the natural and without God is inexplicable.

This story comes from the person directly involved and a miracle can be the only possible explanation. If you can imagine the worst possible high-speed car crash on a motorway. It is carnage, so bad that the engine has been ripped away from its mounting and the dashboard has been pushed right up into the driver's seat. The car is wrecked and in pieces. The roof is buckled, and the floor is a twisted mess. There is no space where someone could sit and still be alive; you would be crushed to death. Yet the driver found himself sitting on the embankment, unable to explain how he got there, and he didn't have a single injury, not a scratch. But what was equally bizarre and difficult to explain was that his boots were missing! These boots were the type you fasten halfway up towards you knee and cannot be removed without significantly loosening off the laces. Where were they? They were tucked deep beneath the driver's seat and still tightly fastened! The other mystery was that he could not have got out of that vehicle without being cut free, so how did he find himself uninjured, alive and sitting 20 feet from his car? His explanation was that God had supernaturally removed him. (The Patient)

As I reflect upon and evaluate my own personal encounter with God's graces and gifts, I hope to better understand the Holy Spirit's role and more truly my experience of Him. I will examine two events where I believe I have ministered in the power of the Holy Spirit and hope to deepen my knowledge and understanding to discern any

46

gifting in these areas. The source of these gifts can be understood from 1 Corinthians 12:4-6 to come from the Triune God according to Paul, when he talks about the same Spirit, Lord and God, but are distributed through the Holy Spirit Himself (1 Cor. 12:11).

A Word of Wisdom

The first experience I wish to discuss I believe involves a speaking gift, a word of wisdom (1 Cor. 12:8). That this only happened once through me confirms this was a word of wisdom for the recipient, a unique supernatural insight into his situation and not mine. The event itself testifies to Jesus' glory and does not promote me or the recipient, further evidence of God's wisdom and involvement (Jn 15:26). [7]Dunn (1975, 79) has described Jesus' own use of charismatic wisdom this way: 'a charismatic insight in particular situations into the will of God'.

On this Sunday morning at Church I sat alongside Rob Fox, a long-standing Christian of more than 30 years. During the service I had what I can only describe as an unappeasable question, to ask Rob if he had ever been baptised as an adult believer (Mk 16:16). What was different about this question was that it felt like it was stuck in the centre of my chest and that it would only go away if I asked it. Rob sat with his eyes closed for an extended time and this only seemed to add to the urgency of this question. Eventually he opened his eyes and I had the opportunity to ask him. To my astonishment he had been praying and asking God this very question. At the next service Rob was baptised and gave his testimony.

The gift of Wisdom is a message communicated to another believer by the Holy Spirit, consistent with truth revealed in scripture and with kingdom ethics. [8]Stibbe describes such revelation as being discerned and not coming from our natural mind. In a theological sense it is related to our belief and in a practical way by our right behaviour in right action (2004, 28).

...his word is in my heart like a fire, a fire shut up in my bones. I am weary of holding it in; indeed, I cannot. (Jeremiah 20:9 NIV)

47

My heart is overflowing with a good theme; (Psalm 45:1)

The Gifts of Healings

Another manifestation of the Spirit is the 'gifts of healings' (1 Cor. 12:8-10). The double plural suggests many kinds of diseases and the different ways in which God heals. [9]Healing can take place in various ways including spiritual, relational, physical, emotional and mental disorders (Pearson 1995, 186).

The healing event I am about to describe took place at the New Wine Summer Conference. Guest speaker Christy Wimber, who pastors the Vineyard Church in Yorba Linda California, expressed a corporate word of faith and prophecy declaring that many in the audience would be set free from illnesses such as depression, anxiety and fear. She invited those who felt this may apply to them to stand up to receive prayer. I felt immediately compelled to pray for a man in his early twenties who had suffered from a long history of panic attacks and anxiety. During the time of prayer, he experienced excessive belching which went on for a considerable length of time. He had only ever experienced an episode like this once before when he was prayed for and completely healed of IBS. At the end of our time together he felt released from his condition.

According to the Gospel of Mark, Jesus could not perform many miracles because of unbelief (Mk. 6:4-6). It is evident from such scripture that faith is associated with the gifts of healings. [10]Stanley (1995, 115-121) describes the gifts of the Spirit as allowing believers to be effective witnesses, to build the body of Christ and to bear fruit. These gifts must be exercised from a position of kingdom authority, allowing the Spirit to manifest His power through us as He chooses. [11]Johnson rightly comments that Jesus commissioned the twelve with the power and authority to minister as He had (2011, 136).

Gifts for today

[12]Cairns (1998, 161) argues a cessationist viewpoint insisting that the Charismata ended in the early Church apostolic period, being the fulfilment of God's revelation and the completion of the New Testament canon. Cairns also noted that every miracle recorded in Acts was associated with the apostles. While this point may be true, [13]Marshall, Travis and Paul (2011, 83, 91) rightly point out that Paul had commended the congregation at Corinth for possessing all the spiritual gifts (1 Cor. 1:7). Cairns also contends that the purpose of the miraculous phenomena was to authenticate the writings of the apostles, but this argument is further weakened as a large section of the New Testament was not written by the apostles at all (Clark 2011, 58). Stibbe (2004, 13) asserts that Paul teaches that the spiritual gifts are for today and are essential until Christ's return. Stanley similarly describes gifts of the Spirit as necessary for effective witness, to produce fruit and to build the body of Christ (1995, 115, 121). Clark (2011, 88-99) sees healing miracles as central to the gospel message and evidence that God's kingdom has been inaugurated, only ceasing at its consummation when Jesus returns (Parousia).

Believers commissioned to heal

Work by [14]Marx (2008, 3) sets out our authority to heal. First Jesus sends out the twelve with authority over *every* sickness, disease and evil spirits (Mt. 10:1). Jesus then sends out the seventy-two with the *same* Kingdom authority (Lk. 10:9, 10:17-20). Jesus has commissioned all believers to obey every command he had given to the apostles (Mt. 28:18-20) which includes healing the sick (Mt 10:7-9).

Conclusion

Many Christians struggle with exercising Spiritual gifts. [15]Ogden (2007, 191) believes that many of us fail to demonstrate Spiritual gifts because of fear, lack of commitment and our past experiences. [15]By a sovereign act of God we receive Charismatic gifts as a form of God's grace (Cantalamessa 2003, 174). I believe that I have once operated the gift of wisdom and many times ministered in the gifts of healings. My theological understanding is that all the Charismata are perpetual and will only cease at the Parousia. Matthew 28:18-20 and Mark 16:15-20 demonstrate that signs will follow believers. Not only has Christ paid for our sins but he has paid for our victory.

Chapter 7 Anecdotes

Working in the ambulance service will involve speaking with people who are hard of hearing or sometimes things are just not heard properly. An example of mishearing what was said could go something like this: "I went into town to pay a check in" and maybe heard or understood as "I went into town to buy a chicken." In that classic film, See no evil. Hear no evil, the character Dave Lyons played by Gene Wilder, gets interrogated by the policeman Braddock. The conversation goes like this, (Braddock) "Was there or wasn't there a woman" (Lyons) "Are you serious?" (Braddock now angered)" Yes I'm serious, was there or wasn't there a woman" (Lyons) "Fuzzy Wuzzy was a woman!"

In the ambulance service, when taking someone's temperature, where possible we would use tympanic thermometers. On one occasion in the back of the ambulance I asked an elderly gentleman if I could take his temperature and pop the thermometer in his ear. He proceeded to stand up and began to unfasten the belt holding up his trousers. I asked him what he was doing, and he replied, "You want to pop it in my rear?" On another occasion I caught part of a conversation between my crew mate and the patient we were attending. Being an amateur musician, I had earlier noticed the upright piano in the adjacent room and my ears pricked up when I thought I heard the mention of a "classical pianist." I joined in the conversation only to discover that what had been said was "cancer of the penis." This chapter is a combination of anecdotes - short stories of my own and some I have heard. You have heard it said that sometimes truth is stranger than fiction!

A dirty act

An ambulance was called to a hair dressing salon in Berkshire. On arrival the crew is presented with a man with lacerations to his head and neck and there is a quantity of matted blood and hair on the floor. A female stylist is sobbing nearby. As the story unfolds, what has happened is truly a 'dirty act'.

Earlier the male customer is seated and puts on a gown to cover his front. At some point the hairdresser notices his hands are moving up and down beneath his gown in a manner to suggest the client is very pleased with his haircut. In disgust, the female stylist takes a mirror and crashes it over the man's head. It soon transpired that this poor man had removed his glasses and was just buffing his 'dirty' glasses below the cape (August 2000 Derek).

A shocking incident

An Oxford ambulance crew were dispatched to an elderly man with a fractured lower arm. The ambulance crew arrived and were directed to the back garden where they find a man supporting his injured limb. "What happened" they ask. "My neighbour hit me with a shovel" he replies. He then goes on to explain that he had been mowing his lawn and at some point, he had picked up a stone in his shoe. He stopped mowing and while holding onto the metal leg of an electric pylon that ran through his back garden, he began to shake his foot with the shoe containing the stone to free it. The neighbour, thinking he was being electrocuted used the nearest object he had, a shovel, to release him from his shocking ordeal, hitting him hard to free him.

I am 'tyred'

A customer took his very nice BMW 3 series to a well know local tyre specialist for four new tyres to be fitted and left it there with the capable young fitters, for a later collection.

Once the tyres were on, the two fitters couldn't resist taking it for a quick spin, at high speed. Woops, they lost control and it ended up rolling onto its roof. Thankfully, no one was hurt but an ambulance crew was sent just in case. Before we left scene, their manager had arrived with two small pink slips in his hand.

Come to collect your car sir? The tyres are fine. We've also carried out an inspection on the underside of your car. Brakes a little iffy but the airbags work...

Posted

Three of us arrived at an address of an Asian family where a man had collapsed. Being in the throes of the Corona virus pandemic we entered the property wearing fluid repellent surgical masks for personal protection, along with gloves and aprons. After a while, the patient had recovered from the collapse and we agreed he should remain at home. We chatted for a while with the family as we completed our records and at some point, a comment was made about how good looking the youngest paramedic was. An older Asian lady said she couldn't tell as we all looked like half letter boxes to her, and everyone roared with laughter. She apologised for her comment which alluded to Boris Johnson's recent burka jibe, but no apology was needed, the delivery was perfectly timed.

Was it a miracle?

Big D and I were given a Doctor's urgent job to take an elderly woman to hospital from a local care home. There was nothing extraordinary about this, but the lady suffered from Aphasia and had no verbal communication following a stroke many years before.

We loaded the patient into the ambulance and offered reassurance even though there came no reply. Now sometimes an ambulance person can get a little bit of a poorly tummy and on this occasion a gassy explosion ensued. The thunderous blast rattled the doors of the ambulance and the ricochet shook the windows. Astonishingly, the lady looked directly at the culprit and exclaimed, "Oh my God". Big D being a sceptic called out "halleluiah, a miracle by my own eyes". Perhaps this should be submitted to a medical research centre for further study. Wind cures mute woman.

Auntie Rita

On this shift there were three of us on the ambulance. Soon after 09:00 am a call came through, known as a concern for welfare call. We were dispatched to a local address about two miles away, to a female in her 70's believed to be collapsed behind closed doors. The call had come from her morning carer who was unable to get a reply from the door and both front and back doors were securely locked. The carer had real cause for concern as the occupant had previously suffered a stroke and had been collapsed in the house on the previous occasion, where access could not be gained. The occupant was my own auntie Rita.

On arrival I instantly recognised the address as that of my auntie Rita. She had net curtains at the windows and most of her curtains were drawn so it was impossible to see into the property, which was a bungalow. We banged on the doors and windows but heard nothing from inside. While all this was taking place two police cars arrived on scene to break entry. The carer's manager also arrived. Outside now were two carers, three ambulance staff and two police officers.

At this time my cousin Michael Rawlings, was on the phone to the morning carer and the phone was passed over to me. Michael assured me that his mum, my auntie, was in the property as she never went anywhere and would most certainly be expecting her morning carer. He was extremely worried. I discussed this with the police officers on scene and strongly suggested they put in the front door, knowing that if my cousin Michael were there, he would have smashed in a window by now, without any hesitation. We all agreed it was the right thing to do.

Out came the door enforcer or the big red key as it is known. Each thud shook the house as he pounded it against the door, which seemed to be totally resistant and would not budge. Instead of the panel breaking in, the frame started cracking and shearing away from the brick work. Again, there was another huge impact to the door and even more damage. The police officer was almost totally spent with effort, but he was determined not to give up. We were all getting ready to run inside, just as a taxi pulled up outside, and sitting in the back was auntie Rita, looking somewhat bemused and perhaps a little angry. "Where have you been?" I asked. "To the hairdressers" she replied. "The good news auntie is, your hair looks lovely, but the bad news......"

Nipples

Chris was having trouble with his ECG sticky tabs placement. After carrying out a twelve lead ECG on a male patient, he started to pull off the leads which were attached by poppers to the ECG dots on the patient's chest. "I'm having real difficulty with this one" Chris proclaimed as he pulled even harder. The patient replied, "that's because you are trying to pop off my left nipple."

Rocky

We drove some 20 miles to a call for concern for welfare to a 101-year-old female whose personal pendant alarm had been activated, but she could not be contacted. There was no answer when we knocked loudly on the front door, which was open. We entered her property to find this little frail old lady in her kitchen preparing food. She was about 4'0" nothing tall. I said "hello it's the ambulance service" but she didn't hear me. I repeated the hello again only this time much louder, but she still couldn't hear me. I made my way over to her and as she caught site of me it startled her. "Get out get out" she screamed. I tried to explain who we were and pointed to our uniforms and my ID badge, but she just kept shouting for us to leave. Next, she started swinging punches at me, a right, and then a left, then an upper cut. Those bony little fists were swinging wildly, for 101 she was in great shape. Luckily for me she didn't knock me out and we left gracefully with no harm done. I'm pretty certain it's the only time I've been beaten up by a 101-year-old.

More Short stories

- You have probably noticed that Big D gets a lot of mention in this book. That's because we were permanent crew mates for several years. One shift, we got asked to check in on a blind woman, who was concerned about her husband upstairs. We arrived without any due concerns and made our way to the back bedroom to find the poor man deceased. He had fallen between his bed and the back wall and was wedged. To get access to him we pulled the bed out and were shocked to see carrier bags stuffed full of thousands of pounds of cash! Any unscrupulous person could have become very rich.

- A crew attended a male patient who castrated himself and flushed his testicles down the toilet.
- Another crew attended a man who over a period of several hours cut off his own arm at the elbow and threw it away.
- We took a man to hospital with a torn anus which he reported happened slipping in the bath onto the taps.
- In 2004 I was the passenger in the ambulance on way to an emergency when we were involved in a crash. No one was hurt.
- One of our paramedics affectionately known as Ginge, was assisting another ambulance services crew on a cardiac arrest. He announced his intension to insert a cannula while CPR continued. Without any warning the student paramedic took it upon her own initiative to administer a shock and Ginge also received 200 joules. I wouldn't describe Ginge as delicate, but I believe his response was, "you better run". He was certainly lucky not to have been killed.

Students, here are some *top tips* for you: Firstly, it goes without saying; please don't defibrillate your fellow ambulance crew mate. Next, sometimes a patient is known as 'code brown'. At times it may be necessary to wrap up the 'code brown' patient tightly in a blanket, them being covered in their own festering faeces of several days. If you are in the back of the ambulance your driver may find it amusing to put on the heaters from the front to heat it up for you and spice up the atmosphere. Tip three; don't be at the bottom of the carry chair when your patient is projectile vomiting. Tip four; don't make someone with severe diarrhoea laugh. Tip five; don't say it's a quiet shift' unless you want to get lynched.

Pet annoyances: When you arrive at an address of a 999 emergency and the patient is waiting outside, with their suitcase already packed in advance and there are three cars sat on the drive. This patient will often tell you they will get seen quicker if they are taken to hospital by ambulance. Another moment of irritation is when you haven't had a break for 8 hours, and the patient greets you with "I just wanted to be checked over". Another irritation, when you get asked, how long have you been an ambulance driver for? Or the patient sat smiling at you and joking around, making telephone calls and sending texts to all their friends while updating their status, and they are telling you their pain score is 10/10. And finally, you turn up at an address on a 999-emergency call and are greeted by the patient whose first words are, "I'm not going to hospital!"

On a more serious note, if you are a student this is a great piece of advice for you, please do remember this. Many newly qualified staff get into the bad habit of believing they must leave as many patients as possible at home, either feeling they are expected to do so, or judging the patient as not warranting hospital admission. Remember this saying, 'if there is any doubt, then there is no doubt, take them to hospital'. If you are leaving them at home, always seek advice from another clinician or GP and be sure that alternate care pathways are in place. It is better to waste a few hours in hospital than to leave someone at home with an uncertain problem.

Risk Adverse or What:

To say the NHS ambulance services pathways algorithm is risk adverse would be downplaying the truth. NHS Pathways are an assessment tool used to triage calls from the public, designed to assess the patient's need for an ambulance. The call takers and 111 staff work tirelessly to assess caller's needs, support people and signpost them to the appropriate care pathway. But it is sometimes the case that a red flag will trigger an emergency response to certain types of incident, often defying logic. Here are a few examples:

Someone with an itchy scalp was dispatched an ambulance for potential anaphylaxis.

Someone with a dry mouth was sent an emergency response for dehydration.

Someone soiled their pants when they broke wind – a 999 response. I believe the medical term is *sharted*. It doesn't get much more serious than this.

A pre-diabetic patient in her 20's threatened to self-harm by drinking coke (and not diet either - scary), because she couldn't access her bank funds.

An emergency response for someone whose toenail came off.

A patient who was constipated, and then did the largest poo I have ever seen. It was a double flusher. (He needed Dyno-Rod, not an ambulance *other drain experts are available).

Dispatched to someone who has vomited, just once.

A patient called 999 for cramp in his leg.

Period pains. Or late on by a couple of days.

Dropped remote control behind sofa.

Couldn't unfasten their belt on their trousers and so on.

Recently, we were sent 29 miles to someone at a walk-in centre to take them just the 300 meters into the ED on the same hospital site. This happens frequently. However, I will finish by noting that many people do call 111 for advice and should been calling 999. The safety netting of the NHS Pathways saves many lives every year.

I hope you have found this chapter to have been light hearted. In the following chapter I will detail some typical day to day incidents you may encounter as an ambulance attendant. Following that, in chapter 9 I will take you through some of the less common and far more extreme incidents I have encountered. In chapter 11 I will tell you about the worst year of my career. Chapter 10, as you will see, is very personal to me.

Chapter 8 – Average days!

I was asked to attend an elderly male, aged 80 years who had fallen from a ladder and had a probable fractured arm. I was attending as a Single Response Vehicle with no available back up at that time. I was out of area at the time of call and was approximately 10 miles from the incident.

On arrival at the patient's address I was escorted to the back of the property by his wife and found the patient seated in the back garden on a chair. He had an obvious fracture to his left humerus as it was grossly deformed with moderate swelling. Before arrival I had requested back up transport via the MTD system.

After greeting the patient and having gained a brief history of events I was able to offer him Entonox for analgesia as there was no history of head or chest injury or any loss of consciousness. His initial pain scoring was 9 out of 10. My patient had fallen from approximately 2'0" off a small set of steps and had landed awkwardly on his left side/arm. Mechanisms for further injury were low and a thorough head to toe assessment demonstrated no other injuries other than a small abrasion over his left elbow. There was no indication for spinal immobilisation.

There was no external haemorrhaging as the fracture was closed. Circulation and nerve function were normal at the site and distal to the injury. I now had time to take further observations, gain IV access to provide Morphine for better pain management and to enable fracture immobilisation. I accomplished this by splinting his arm to his body using triangular bandages tied together. His pain score was now 7 out of 10. Other observations included a blood pressure of 125/75, a pulse rate of 80 regular and a respiratory rate of 18 breaths per minute. There was no paraesthesia or pallor to the limb and circulation was normal. This elderly gentleman had no other medical history other than gall stones and was not on any prescribed medication.

Regular updates from control via the telephone informed me that no back up transport was going to be available for some time. I had been on scene for over 45 minutes and my patient was now comfortable under the circumstances. After considering all my options and following the current policy/guidelines on categories of patients who are suitable for transportation by a single response vehicle, I liaised with control and we agreed that it was appropriate to transport this patient in the SRV. On arrival at hospital the receiving staff nurse sent him to Triage.

We were on emergency area cover at High Wycombe ambulance station and were paged to attend a 42-year-old male from a nearby address with chest pains. Further details were sent en-route to include a known cardiac history and chest pains today not relieved by patient's own glyceryl trinitrate spray (GTN). Time to arrival on scene was 5 minutes.

On arrival I was led to my patient by his family. As I approached my patient my initial impression was that he looked well but was clearly anxious. This gentleman was of Asian ethnicity and currently I was taking lessons in Urdu at Aylesbury College. My tutor there had been encouraging me to greet Muslims in the traditional way, assuring me that it would be well received. As I approached my patient, I said hello and then followed with the greeting of *as-salāmu alaikum* which means 'Peace be upon you'. Although surprised my patient's demeanour had changed and he was now smiling, he reached out to shake my hand and replied *alaikum as-alām* which translates to 'and to you peace'. I felt that this simple greeting had helped to remove any cultural barriers.

I now began to take a comprehensive history and make a complete patient assessment. He informed me that he had had a coronary artery bypass graft (CABG) for a single vessel 5 years earlier and had remained well until recently. He went on to say that he had experienced central chest pains just 4 days previously and was transferred to the Hammersmith hospital in London where a stent was done the following day to the right coronary artery. He was then discharged that same day. He also had a history of being insulin dependent diabetic for 9 years. Today he was experiencing a sharp central chest pain which did not radiate. The pain had started suddenly, and he had taken his GTN spray straight away. Pain was not altered by movement or respiration in any way. His family called the ambulance after 10 minutes as the pain remained the same and they were deeply concerned.

I gave my patient reassurance as we continued to treat him and take further clinical observations. Initial observations were as follows: Pulse rate of 64 beats per minute regular and full. Respiratory rate was 16 breaths per minute with no shortness of breath, no cough and clear lung sounds on auscultation – Spo2 95% on room air. His initial blood pressure reading was 140/80 mmHg. Blood sugar reading was 5.6 mmol. The 12 lead ECG recording showed slight S-T segment depression in leads 3 & 4. The patient had first scored his pain at 10/10. After the administration of 10mg IV morphine sulphate, 300mg of aspirin and 500 mcg glyceryl trinitrate his pain score was now 7/10; this did not alter any further. His colour remained good; he had not experienced any nausea or vomiting and was not sweating.

We treated this patient for an acute coronary syndrome and transported him to the nearest appropriate facility to deal with his condition. A pre-alert was given, and he was transported with lights and with sirens when needed. Time from call to being in A&E was just 36 minutes.

We were dispatched from the ambulance station to attend the address of a 62-year-old male with a laceration to his foot. As further details were received through the MTD system we learnt that the patient was also haemophiliac and a wheelchair user. We soon arrived at the address and went to the back of the property as we had been directed. On entering I introduced myself and my colleague and we started to gain a history of events. This patient's primary concern was that he was unable to stem the bleeding albeit only slight because of his blood clotting disorder. The bleed had been ongoing for approximately 5 hours and he had sought advice from the haemophiliac centre in Oxford who in turn had contacted the on-call medics at Stoke Mandeville Hospital. He informed us that Stoke Hospital was expecting him and they would be able to administer the factor IV injection known as the Christmas factor, needed to stop the bleeding and to produce a clotting effect.

On examination the laceration between his toes was relatively small. The laceration was approximately 1cm in length between the fourth and fifth metatarsals of his left foot. After the examination of the injured area it was evident that a detailed history was necessary as this patient had limited sensation due to his disability. He reported that he had caught his foot under the front of his wheelchair which was motorised and was clearly weighty (approximately 150Lbs). Respectfully I asked him the reason why he used a wheelchair and if he had any sensation at all. He reported his disability is due to a condition caused by a syndrome called Charcot-Marie-Tooth disease (CMT) known also as Charcot-Marie-Tooth neuropathy, hereditary motor and sensory neuropathy (HMSN). It is characterized by loss of muscle tissue and touch sensation, predominantly in the feet and legs but also in the hands and arms in the advanced stages of disease.

This man's legs were very flaccid and malformed, and it was apparent that the condition was well advanced. He had reduced sensation. He informed us that he had been diagnosed with the condition in his late teen years. Wasting of muscle tissue in the lower parts of the legs, a high arch of the foot and hammer toe are common signs and were clearly seen on examination and would make any assessment more difficult. I was also concerned because he has a much higher risk of bleeding which could also complicate any undisclosed injury. A closer examination did not reveal any other obvious wounds, no deformity was seen or crepitus felt and no visible contusion. A good strong pedal pulse could be palpated, capillary refill was normal, and the skin colour and temperature were also as expected. Our treatment strategy currently was to apply a wound dressing and elevate the limb where possible to reduce the bleeding.

Did You Know Section:

Did you know: If someone has been immobile and laying on the floor for more than 4 hours they should be seen in hospital? This is known as Rhabdomyolysis. Lying on the floor for long periods can result in a rapid breakdown of muscle. If this occurs and isn't treated it can lead to an acute kidney injury or permanent damage.

Did you know that if someone who has apparently fainted (TLoC) *and* been urinary incontinent, that they should be seen in hospital? Do they remember falling? Further investigation should be carried out.

Did you know when someone has a brain injury such as a stroke, their eyes may be fixed looking up and across to the side of the brain where the injury is.

Did you know a thunderclap headache may be a symptom of a life-threatening condition such as a bleed on the brain? There may also be nausea, vomiting or loss of consciousness.

Did you know, if a child has hit their head and has symptoms of persistent vomiting, normally more than three episodes, they will normally require a CT scan.

Common incidents attended:

- Respiratory distress / breathing problems
- Chest pain
- Abdominal pain
- Falls
- Trauma
- Seizures including febrile convulsion
- Mental health and psychiatric disorders
- Deliberate self-harm including suicide
- Stroke / cerebral haemorrhage
- Diabetic problems
- Arrhythmias. Cardiac rhythm disturbances / cardiac arrest
- Overdose and deliberate self-harm
- Neck of femur fracture (NOF)
- PV bleeding (per-vaginal)
- Maternity and obstetric incidents
- Allergy and anaphylaxis
- Road traffic collisions
- Social and welfare concerns

Pause for thought: How can inanimate matter organise itself to contemplate itself?

-Allan Sandage

(Lee Strobel. The Case for Faith. Page 92)

Maternity 1:

We were called to attend a 23-year-old female in labour, gestation 40 weeks and it was reported that her contractions were coming approximately every 1 to 2 minutes. With this information we requested via control the attendance of a midwife who would be the appropriate professional *specialist*. On arrival at the patient's address we were greeted by a very anxious father who directed us to his wife. This lady was laid recumbent on the lounge floor and a quick assessment showed that she was in stage two labour, as the baby's head was clearly visible at the vulva. After introducing myself and my colleague I offered our patient Entonox (gas and air) for pain relief which she rapidly accepted. The Entonox works twofold by providing analgesia for pain relief and an increase in oxygenation. We prepared the maternity pack, assisted our patient into a more comfortable position, provided blankets for modesty where possible and placed some Inco-pads under our patient to protect the surroundings. During this time, we also established her medical and maternal history and took our first set of base line observations.

Throughout the delivery process I continually reassured her and provided correct clinical support throughout. Our patient reported that her waters had broken at 11:15 hours today. This was a planned home delivery and was the patient's second child. The contractions had only started at 20:35 hours this evening and things had really started to happen at around 21:00 hours. We were called to attend at 21:07 hours and arrived on scene at 21:22hours. Within just eight minutes the baby was delivered safely at 21:30 hours. I wrapped and dried the baby and placed it on the mother's abdomen. There were no obvious signs of perineal tearing or of significant haemorrhaging. It was at this time the midwife arrived on scene and took over the patient's management. The patient was documented as G2 + P2 which means she has had 2 pregnancies resulting in 2 births. We gave the neonate (new-born baby) an Apgar score of 9 at 1 minute being:

I.   Heart rate above 100 beats/min = 2
II.   Respiratory effort, crying   = 2
III.   Muscle tone, active motion   = 2
IV.   Colour, pink body and blue extremities = 1
V.   Reflex irritability to stimulus = 2
   Total APGAR score 9

On reflection all had gone well. We had been called due to the sudden and unexpectedly fast delivery of the baby which hadn't been anticipated and also for the provision of pain relief. This family were some distance from any local hospital and the midwife was presently not available. Being a planned home birth, it was of course expected to happen without any significant complications and all the necessary checks and safety nets would have been explored by the midwifery and allied medical teams to ensure that any risks were minimal. Having said that, I still feel uncomfortable and worried when attending labour incidents as clearly this field has its own highly trained professionals who are better equipped to deal with complications and have a vast experiential knowledge. Ambulance personnel attend very few home births. In 23 years, I have delivered around 15 healthy babies.

It is fair to say that most pregnant women are healthy, and that childbirth is usually a happy event. By this time of course, an amazing new life has undergone an incredible journey.

Pause for thought: *For you created my inmost being; you knit me together in my mother's womb. (Psalm 139: 13-14)*

Maternity 2:

With any imminent birth, it's always good practice en-route to check in with EOC (emergency operations control), and request the attendance of a midwife. This property was some distance from any hospital or maternity facility. On this occasion we only had a house name and in 2001 we had no access to satellite navigation (GPS) but relied on map reading. I asked control to inquire the exact location from the caller, which proved to be a great help.

On attending the patient, I offered Entonox for pain relief. At this point the patient asked for something stronger for the pain. I explained that this was all we were able to offer for pain relief during labour. The patient's husband then interrupted and informed us that he had some pethidine and asked us to administer it to his wife. Pethidine is an opiate based pain-relieving drug carried by midwifes given as an intramuscular injection.

I explained to the husband that we had no protocol allowing us to administer this drug. The husband then suggested he was a registered GP and that if we could supply him with a syringe and needle, he would administer the drug himself. His statement seemed untruthful, so I questioned him a little further, at which point he backed down and admitted he was in no way medically trained. He did go on to say however, that his own father would be arriving shortly with a syringe and needle and he would then administer the drug himself at that time. I strongly advised against this and suggested this would be very foolish and that we were totally against the idea. Fortunately, the baby arrived very soon after and before this could happen. I documented the details on the patient report form.

The birth itself was another pre-planned home delivery, which are generally safe but still have the scope for things to go wrong. The patient and his wife had their own agenda – the midwife was some distance away and we were presented with a couple whose expectations were not going to be fully met. At that time, had the patient suffered a post-partum haemorrhage, paramedics did not carry the drug of choice Syntometrine, used by midwives to manage bleeding by causing the uterus to contract. With some 5% of deliveries resulting in post-partum haemorrhage, defined as blood loss of 500 ml or more, this was always a worry for ambulance crews. It is also worth mentioning that not all ambulances have a paramedic in attendance and are often a technician crew. Today expectant mothers have greater choices over birth settings and with a national shortage of midwives' paramedics are being called more frequently to attend maternity incidents.

Obstetric emergency:

We were called to attend a 24-year-old female who had collapsed at home. On our arrival we found her lying on her side on her bathroom floor, looking extremely pallid but having no signs of external haemorrhage. She reported some abdominal discomfort and feeling light-headed. One of the first questions I asked this younger female was if there any possibility you could be pregnant.

We took some basic observations, but they were far from normal. Her blood pressure was very low, in fact almost not recordable, but what was confusing was that her heart rate remained steady at exactly 50 beats per minute. This was not what you would expect. Normally, if a haemorrhage was a cause for collapse, the heart tries to compensate by speeding up in rate, thereby increasing more blood and oxygen to the tissues. She was profoundly bradycardic, and a cardiac cause just didn't fit the presentation. Her ECG was normal.

This young woman denied being pregnant and reported that she had miss-carried only a few weeks earlier. At that time, she also underwent dilation and curettage, a medical procedure used to clear the uterus (womb) of tissue following a miss-carriage. We treated her for suspected blood loss and placed a cannula in her arm located at the antecubital fossa, and set up fluids, which were administered judiciously. We made a priority call to Stoke Mandeville hospital and she went into the resuscitation room on our arrival. We learnt a few days later that she was taken to theatre for emergency surgery because she had ruptured her fallopian tube, caused by a missed ectopic pregnancy. Behind her womb was trapped 3 litres of blood. This blood had been pressing against her vagal nerve causing her heart rate to slow down, known as a vagal response. This was very unusual, but I wonder if this saved her life; a slower heart rate would not push blood so aggressively into the cavity behind her womb, perhaps reducing overall blood loss.

Pause for thought: The heavens declare the glory of God. Psalm 91

Music:

Have you ever just lain on your back staring up at the stars and enjoying their majesty? There becomes a sense of awe. It has been well documented that a cosmic hum can be detected, as though the universe itself is speaking to us or even perhaps singing. Or perhaps the smallest of structures has given you an incredible but indescribable sense of magnificence. What in life for you has given you great joy?

For many people music holds a special place in their inner being. It can stir up our emotions and alter our mood or bring a flood of memories, good or bad. Music is an important part of life and can be a tool to communicate. For me, I love the sound of the saxophone with its expressive vocal quality and rich dynamics. I would go even further to say that its entire shape pleases me with all the intricate rods and key work. An old saxophone in bare brass from years of wear excites me even further as something about the darker aged brass with its patina brings a sense of time and history.

The saxophone was invented by the Belgium born instrument maker Adolphe Sax where it takes its name. As complex as this instrument's structure appears, nobody in their right mind would argue that it came about by chance or sheer luck. It didn't create itself. Someone had to conceive of it in their mind and construct it, right? Yet we see in nature the most beautiful designs of such immense complexity but argue it is there by chance. How can chaos order itself?

In the bible the number 8 represents new beginning and in music the 8th note is a new beginning of the repeated scale or octave. The fingerprints of the creator are all over music. All the way through the bible is the recurrence of the number seven, known as the heptadic structure. Seven is called the number of God and represents something as being complete, much like a musical diatonic scale. It also represents perfection. Incidentally, there are seven colours in a rainbow. The God of creation invites you to experience Him through music and through the natural world with all your senses.

Psalm 95: let us make a joyful noise to the rock of our salvation!

Chapter 9 – Not so Average Days

Pause for thought: Fear is the opposite of faith

Sometimes you will arrive at the scene of a serious event and there is utter silence, no one says a single word, but you can see the visible anguish on faces. Other times people are in complete shock and even denial that anything is wrong, they appear to be totally unaware or deny that their family member has stopped breathing, even as you start CPR and deliver shocks from the defibrillator. On other occasions you will encounter complete despair and hear howling, screaming and pleading for a reversal in truth. I have seen people in so much emotional pain and despair that they have hurled themselves prostrate to the floor, utterly inconsolable, there are no words of comfort to find.

As an ambulance person you will need to be a very physical presence for that person. Detachment is not always easy in these terrible circumstances; you are only human and having friends and family of your own, your personal feelings may impact you strongly. Being a carer for others can bring great sadness as you bear witness to their outpouring of grief. Events involving death or serious injury and events where there is a feeling of wanting to have done more are likely to result in a greater impact upon your mental health. [1]A traumatic event is exposure to or encountering an incident that causes emotional, physical, psychological distress or harm. It may include exposure to death, threatened death, actual or threatened serious injury or threatened or actual violence of a sexual nature. Reactions may include exhaustion, confusion, inappropriate guilt, sadness, anxiety, agitation, confusion, intrusive thoughts, feeling numb and so on.

[2]Sometimes it is necessary to hold a debriefing after such cases and even find support for ourselves. It may be important for you to access good social support or professional help. Traumatic stress reactions are often acute

reactions following the immediate aftermath of an incident and may be experienced intensely. It is possible you may experience emotional, cognitive, physical and behavioural responses, resulting in potentially multiple physical effects. Traumatic stress reactions that are considered normal often include re-experiencing or re-living what happened, avoidance or staying away from reminders, hyper arousal or feeling anxious or jumpy, difficulty with sleeping or nightmares for example. In my own career my personal experience has been to go to an emotional place I never knew existed. If you are going to join the ambulance service at any level and stay in this role for many years, I believe you are likely, at some point, to experience some level of these intense emotions.

Statement regarding an Incident:

At 12:51 I was passed an incident via the car MDT I was deployed to work on, (NR210) for an unconscious 68-year-old female for a potential cardiac arrest. I was first to arrive on scene before any other ambulance resources. I was unable to get any response at the front door of the property which was locked so I carried my equipment to the rear door which I found to be open. I shouted for a location and made my way upstairs to where I found the patient's husband carrying out CPR on the patient on the bedroom floor. I asked him if he was able to continue with the chest compressions while I attached defib pads. Patient B was in Asystole. I was informed by the husband that the patient had been suffering with severe abdominal pain the day before and this continued through to today, she had been struggling to walk on both days. Initially it was unclear when he had last seen her alive, but he stated later that he had last checked in on her about two hours earlier, believing her to have been sleeping.

The second resource soon arrived on scene and donned level 3 PPE. The second crew set up the Lucas device bought to scene by Team Leader 'Little Daz'. I cannulated the patient and started the first round of IV adrenaline. Once it was deemed necessary to move to an advanced airway adjunct the care of the patient at this point was continued by the second private resource that were assisting. Her prognosis remained very poor as she was believed to have been in cardiac arrest for an extended period before our arrival.

I and little Daz continued to support the crew and the patient's husband over the duration of the resuscitation attempt. After all possible efforts were made to resuscitate the patient, on advice from our Medical Incident Advisor life was pronounced extinct and CPR stopped. I had been made aware that the patient had been seen the day before by a SCAS crew, but this information was passed to me by Daz, not the patient's husband.

I informed control that the patient was deceased and asked them to contact TVP (Thames Valley Police) following local protocol. I and Daz kept the patient's husband informed as to the processes in such events following an unexpected death. The patient's husband remained in deep emotional shock and we felt he was struggling to cope, so we suggested he could perhaps find some support from his close neighbour.

I next spoke with TVP Police Sergeant Day (not real name) who was satisfied that a police representative did not need to attend the scene. Following this in line with procedure I next phoned the patient's own GP. I spoke to Dr White from a local surgery at this point who has just moments earlier tried to ring the patient's home telephone as they had contacted the surgery that morning for a call back. Dr White was deeply shocked and saddened with the news that the patient had died, and he reported that he had known her for more than 30 years. Dr White was audibly upset. He stated that the patient had probably died from a perforated bowel and that he will probably be required to write a coroner's report.

Before I left scene after offering my deepest condolences, the undertakers had already arrived to remove the patient from the address. On my return to the ambulance station I completed a Datix report as directed to do so by Daz. What I found most distressing was not only had this poor man lost his wife and a future with her, but within 90 minutes of her death she was gone from their home and he would never lay eyes on her again.

Helicopter crash:

It was the middle of winter, now very cold outside and just starting to get dark. Loudly and without warning the station red phone rang, sounding throughout the entire ambulance station as it was connected to a network of speakers. Our instructions from the control room dispatcher were to drive to the helipad where a police helicopter was about to land. The so-called helipad is a small piece of grass in a field just across the road from the ambulance station, behind a community hall. Our task was to pick up a male patient who had earlier crashed a private helicopter and sustained a very serious laceration across his entire throat, almost from ear to ear. The patient was prone (face down) on a scoop stretcher and was accompanied by an ambulance technician and a police officer from the Amersham area.

All was satisfactory in the ambulance; the patient was warm, stable and breathing normally. His prone position allowed his wound to drain away naturally any secretions by gravity. He was wearing a thick tunic coat and there was no reason to remove it or give him any further medical attention. As we drove him the 2 minutes to the hospital ED, we phoned through to make sure the trauma team was standing by and ready to receive him.

Waiting for us in the ED were a huge clinical team of 15 plus staff including a surgeon and an anaesthetist? I think probably some of the staff who had come in where only there out of morbid curiosity just to have a look. After a comprehensive handover from the Amersham ambulance technician we slid the patient, still prone on our scoop, onto the resuscitation room hospital bed. All was well and he was now safely in the care of the trauma team!

Perhaps I should have challenged what happened next and spoken up! The patient's condition was clear for all to see and it is not easy for a paramedic to question an experienced anaesthetist whose field of expertise is airway management. In addition to this, there was also a surgeon in-situ who would surely interject if needed? So, when the anaesthetist decided to roll the patient onto his back, me and my crew mate Chris gave each other a surprised look and muttered under our breath something like 'that's definitely a bad idea'.

This was a huge mistake; no one had made an adequate assessment of his airway, and there was no cannula inserted into his arm. What followed was like something out of a comedy horror, only there was nothing funny about it, the patient lost his airway and ability to breathe.

This man was terrified and panicking. As he tried his hardest to sit up because he was unable to breathe, staff were trying their hardest to push him back down flat onto the bed, this only adding to his utter panic. Another clinician was trying to get hold of his arm and put in a cannula, but he was now starting to become combative as his brain was beginning to starve of oxygen. The patient forcibly pushes those around him away. His colour changes from red to purple while his bulging eyes seem to be screaming 'please help me'. The bewildered anaesthetist has in his hand a suction yankaur which is sucking the surrounding air, hoping to get an opportunity to suction out the man's airway but seems unsure about what he can do.

Next comes the part that is bizarre, the patient is pointing frantically at the suction yankaur and then pointing to his mouth, urging the anaesthetist to suck out his airway. Moments later the patient grabs the suction out of the anaesthetist's hand and rams it down his own throat, suctioning his own airway, all this seemingly taking more time than you can imagine someone not breathing to have. At last someone managed to get a cannula into his lower leg or ankle, and they administer a drug to put him to sleep. It then took around a further five minutes to secure his airway before he could be given adequate ventilation. He went to theatre. I have no idea of his outcome.

Stabbing and Award:

We were dispatched to attend a 17-year-old male with stab wounds to his sternum/chest and abdomen. His bowel was protruding which we covered with cling film and he had a potential sucking wound to his chest which we protected with a chest seal. He was given 1gm of Tranexamic acid, a clotting agent to protect from concealed bleeding. His initial heart rate was 150bpm with no palpable radial pulse. He remained agitated and clammy. In hospital he was given warmed blood and plasma, and an ultrasound scan revealed a large cardiac tamponade compressing his left ventricle. He also had a suspected intra-abdominal bleed.

On Monday 18th February 2019 I received a High Sheriff's award for recognition of professionalism and skilled actions taken to save the life of this 17-year-old man wounded in Aylesbury on 14th June 2018. These actions were a joint effort from me, Sarah Catchpole and Juliet McGill and others. The ceremony took place at Aylesbury Crown Court and was presented by His Honour Judge Sheridan and Professor Ruth Farwell CBE (High Sheriff of Buckinghamshire). This incident wasn't by any means difficult, but the award for me felt like recognition for the many years of other significant and difficult incidents I attended throughout my career.

Woman with knife incident:

It was 2019 and I was working with Stephen Thomas on an early shift. At the beginning of our shift we were asked to assist another crew who were attending the scene of a 34-year-old female who had reported feeling suicidal. We arrived on scene at 06:32am and received an initial handover form the night crew. Prior to our arrival this crew had to withdraw from the property as the patient became challenging and refused help. The crew felt that at that time the patient was lacking mental capacity. The patient had reported to them that she had earlier taken cocaine. The first crew had requested attendance from the police as they were concerned about the threats the patient had made.

As I stepped from the first crew's ambulance having received a handover, I noticed the patient and a male companion had come out of the property to smoke. It was disclosed that the male was her brother. I introduced myself to the patient and started a conversation with her to see if we were able to help her with her situation. She seemed calm and she asked me if she could speak with me privately, so I led her to my ambulance. At this point the first crew left scene as they had finished their shift.

The patient sat on the rear facing seat and I left the ambulance side door open for her reassurance and my own safety. She then disclosed that her boyfriend had wanted to kill her brother. I asked her more about this and she reported it had to do with other threats she had received from another person. During this period of assessment I felt that she was now demonstrating mental capacity and could therefore decide for herself whether or not she should go to hospital, although it was stressed to her that it was in her best interest to go. She said she would not go so I asked her to sign our electronic record to record and confirm her decision. She signed twice, once for the refusal and a second time confirming that she had received a full assessment. She then left the ambulance and went back inside the property.

Stephen and I sat in the back of the ambulance to finish completing our electronic patient report. A few minutes later at 06:48am the patient returned and standing by the side door which had remained open, she demanded we should leave. She reported her brother whose property we were outside, didn't want us to stay any longer. I explained that we would need a further 15 minutes to finish paperwork, to stand down the police, and to explain to our control room that we were acting in her best interest and discharging her at scene. I explained that this was all being done for her and was what she had wanted. I also pointed out that we were on a public road and were not obliged to move away. She then stated that she would get a knife and stab me if I didn't leave immediately.

The patient returned to the property and I slammed up the side door and asked Stephen to lock the vehicle with us inside the back of the ambulance. We both double checked that the doors were locked. Just a few moments later she reappeared at the side door frantically trying to open it and stabbing wildly at the door itself. I could see in her right hand a large steel chef's slicing knife with an 8-inch blade. I prepared the camera on the electronic patient report device and shouted at her to show me what she had in her hand. She raised her arm with the knife in her hand and I snapped a picture with the camera. I next radioed control asking for immediate police assistance explaining our situation. The police arrived 15 minutes later, and she was arrested and taken into custody. She appeared before High Wycombe's magistrates Court where she pleaded guilty to the following charge: Threatening a person with a blade / sharp pointed article in a public place.

Takotsubo patient outside theatre:

In cases of intense emotional stress or bereavement a person can experience acute heart failure and sudden death. This is known as takotsubo cardiomyopathy or 'broken heart syndrome'. The wall of the left ventricle of the heart is suddenly weakened and changes shape and this in turn affects the hearts ability to pump well. This rare phenomenon can occur after the loss of someone. This has been recorded after the loss of a spouse or lifelong partner, and they both end up dying within days of each other. I and another crew attended a 45-year-old female who suddenly dropped down suffering such a cardiac event; also, as she fell, she hit her head on the curb and suffered a traumatic bleed on her brain. An ultrasound scan of her heart showed takotsubo syndrome. She was successfully resuscitated and walked out of the John Radcliffe hospital a few weeks later. Her emotional stress before the event had been massive.

Gunshot injuries:

Deneen Shaw and I were called to a local address just half a mile from the ambulance station which is based at Stoke Mandeville hospital. A man aged 33 years was reported to have been shot three times and armed police were now on scene. It was later reported that an off-duty police officer had heard the gun shots at approximately 09:55 hours that morning but the victim wasn't found until 10:44 hours.

We were directed to the hallway of the property where the patient was lying on the floor. He was a wheelchair user who had previously been shot in the back and paralysed some years earlier. We learnt that the address he was at was a 'safe house' as he was in a witness protection scheme. This was an assassination attempt that had failed. The patient had been shot in both arms. I had imagined that as he was probably trying to protect his head from the bullets or maybe he had been shot in his arms to disable him. The third bullet was fired behind his left ear and had travelled through to the opposite side of his skull. Amazingly he was able to move about but was combative and trying to fight us as we tried to help him, including biting and lashing out, so it became necessary to cuff his hands to manage him safely. On the vinyl tiled floor was approximately 700 millilitres of blood. He scored a Glasgow Coma Scale of 10.

After the patient was put into an induced coma in the resuscitation room at Stoke hospital, Deneen and I were asked to blue light him to the John Radcliffe Hospital with a full escort team including an anaesthetist, operating department practitioner and police. This was the only time I have ever seen such an event unfold like this. We had police officers in the back of the ambulance, two-armed response vehicle to escort us on our journey, one in front and one behind us. As we arrived at Headington in Oxford every major road that joined our route was blocked off by police cars to ensure our safe and rapid journey. Whatever this man had been involved in, there was still a serious concern that the assassin may be at large and ready to finish off this attempted murder.

Here is a brief list I have made of some less day-to-day jobs I have attended over a three-year period from 2018 to 2020.

12 patients at a school inhaled Bromine from a science lab mishap. Multiple crews in attendance 03/2018.

A 74-year-old female having an Addison's crisis. Given Hydrocortisone 03/2018

40-year-old male crushed under his own car when the jack slipped. Helimed in attendance 06/2018

41-year-old male with serious chest trauma after falling off scaffolding. Trauma call 07/2018

80-year-old male cardiac arrest at a care home. Patient was a tracheostomy (neck breather) patient. I intubated him through his stoma, and we got a return of spontaneous circulation 11/2018

31-year-old man crashed car while high on cocaine and intoxicated (EtOH). Combative and extremely challenging patient requiring police assistance 03/2019

18-year-old male with maxillofacial injuries after coming off his push bike. He had no brakes and used his foot against the front wheel, then went over the handlebars. He lost several teeth and large part of his mouth and flesh around his eyeball 04/19.

33-year-old male fell of a building roof top 60 feet high and landed on his feet, having bilateral lower leg fractures 06/2019

24-year-old male in cardiac arrest. Successfully resuscitated after 17 defibrillation shocks. Went onto ECMO and was expected to go on heart transplant list. 10/2019

80-year-old male with dextrocardia 10/2019.

36-year-old male cardiac arrest. Prolonged resuscitation on scene with helicopter crew also in attendance, but sadly died. 10/2019

49-year-old female fatal motorbike traumatic arrest. Double chest drains and needle chest decompression. Sadly, died on scene. 07/2020

68-year-old male fell from upstairs bedroom window. Traumatic arrest. Attended in full level 3 PPE. Massive head injury sadly died on scene. 09/2020.

Chapter 10 - Contaminated Blood

Pause for thought: Grief in the price you pay for love (HMQE II)

In this chapter I would like to take you back in time to 1979[1]. My friend Joe Huitson and I were just 13 years of age, Margaret Thatcher had become the first female Prime Minister, Sid Vicious of the Sex Pistols had died after a heroin overdose, the so called Yorkshire Ripper is at large and Roger Moore stars in the eleventh James Bond movie Moonraker. Significantly the economy has shrunk by 2.3% for the third quarter of the year; inflation rises by 13.4% with lending rates at an all-time high. To add to this the government cuts public spending by £3.5 billion. But 13-year-old boys don't have time to worry about all this; there was too much mischief to be had and surely the authorities of a so called 'first world' country being so advanced in medical care could do no harm? We had no way of knowing how this notion was far from reality in truth. In fact, by now Joe was probably already a sufferer of the biggest scandal and treatment disaster in NHS history.

We were typically bored on a hot summer's day and looking for something to do. At age thirteen you don't really think much about the consequences of the high-spirited behaviour you find yourself doing, so what could really go wrong jumping from garage roof to garage roof? This would be harmless fun and if any adult should challenge us, we were masters of avoiding capture – we could run for it. I wasn't really paying too much attention as Joe was walking backwards ready for his big jump. I turned to see him, but he had already disappeared out of sight, so I walked over to the edge of the garages to find him lying on his back, some 7'0" below. He seemed ok but was complaining he had broken his ankle. At first, I was a little suspicious, thinking it was just another foolish prank but doubt soon turned into concern as I started to realise, he had hurt himself. Joe growing up was a force to be reckoned with, being both incredibly strong physically and mentally resilient; he was a human dynamo. But he did have a serious problem; he suffered with the congenital medical condition haemophilia, a blood clotting disorder.

After sitting there for around 10 minutes Joe's pain seemed to settle as endorphins, our body's natural pain reliever had seemed to numb his injury. Joe was now sure he had only sprained his ankle, so we decided to stand and try and walk home. Once Joe put his full weight on his foot he yelled out in pain as he caused further injury to the serious fracture dislocation he already had, now causing a puncture through the skin. He somehow managed to hop to a nearby road and almost immediately a young woman pulled up in her car, seeing the situation we were in she kindly took us to Joe's home address. After sitting at home for about 30 minutes with no adult help around we decided to call for an ambulance, as by now the pain was becoming unbearable. The ambulance attendant, no doubt an ambulance technician at that time, placed his lower leg and ankle into a box splint and Joe went off to hospital in the ambulance by himself. He was later transferred to the Nuffield Orthopaedic hospital in Oxford, for specialist care for the injury he had sustained and for his haemophilia. Joe spent around six weeks in hospital and was most likely given factor VIII injections (anti-haemophilic factor), an essential blood clotting agent that would help his blood to clot. This wasn't the first time Joe had received factor VIII and wouldn't be the last either.

Haemophilia is a congenital condition that affects the bloods ability to clot. Thousands of haemophiliacs and other patients who received blood transfusions in the 1970-80's where given contaminated blood products and this is where this shocking scandal begins. You may ask why this story is being told in this book, a book about the ambulance service, paramedic practice and faith. The answer is; to acknowledge the pain, grief and bereavement experienced by everyone who has ever lost someone they love. All the accounts given in this entire book are true stories and behind many of them is real heartache. I wish to honour those relationships and lives. I wish to give account of the life of an incredible man and advocate in his memory the accountability still required for his death. I want to bring to your attention the story of this 'contaminated blood' NHS scandal.

The haemophilia society[2] report that more than 4,689 haemophiliacs have been infected with HIV and hepatitis viruses from factor concentrates containing these lethal diseases. As early as 1975 there was serious concern from medical practitioners that blood imported from America could be lethal. Many recipients' only found out years later they had contracted these diseases after their health began to deteriorate, caused by this cocktail of toxic drugs. Additionally, many other people who had received blood transfusions were also infected. These included mothers who had just given birth and children who were receiving treatment for leukaemia (ITV News Meridian 21.02.22). Since this systemic NHS catastrophe began at least 3000 are now known to have died.

ITV News Meridian (24.01.22) has also reported on an enquiry into the Treloar's boarding School near Alton, Hampshire, UK, which in the 1980's had an NHS haemophilia centre onsite. These young pupils were also given the same toxic contaminated blood products, which included imported blood donated by prisoners, sex workers and drug addicts in America for a cash payment. This pooling together of plasma from thousands of donors guaranteed infection for the recipient. Out of 100 infected pupils only 17 now survive. [3]In April 2017 Labour MP Andy Burnham, in the House of Commons described the contaminated blood scandal as "a criminal cover up, on an industrial scale". In the UK, to date no one has yet been held responsible.

You will recall Joe's childhood story above. 40 years and six children later, Joe has loved life to its fullest even though he had been plagued with many health issues and illnesses. Joe was one of many people who were infected with contaminated blood containing hepatitis C which ultimately led to liver cirrhosis, liver cancer with metastatic spread and his premature death. He had many bleeds in his joints as he went through life because the contaminated blood had caused a complex immune system response affecting his blood clotting further. In June 2020 Joe had severe back pain and within only a few days had lost his ability to walk. Within three months he was paralysed from the diaphragm down. Even then he remained positive; determined to live well with whatever time he had, never being defined by his illness. His legacy for me was his sheer joy of life. Not for one second had he let his many health issues stop his irrepressible nature and dampen his ability to live fully. He fronted bands as a singer, worked tirelessly for those less fortunate in life and dedicated himself to his family.

In no way is there ever any real justice in this life for anyone who has ever lost someone they love through negligence, trauma or premature death. In fact, any loss of a close relationship leaves us in pain and with a deep sense of loss and wanting. There are no words that could ever make this grief less painful or loss less significant. We have or will all lose someone we love, and I am mindful that what I write are real situations that are filled with despair and hurt. In this book I share my own personal experiences as a paramedic of more than 23 years and some of the incidents are also very personal to me. When we are grieving for someone it is often hard to remember that person before their illness. But I encourage you to remember there was a life you can celebrate and a relationship to recall. What were those things that were important to them in life, their achievements, their way of being and living? How will their character and personality be remembered?

Everyone feels loss and grief at some point in their life. However, this book includes accounts of my own Christian experience and walk with God and how my faith and relationship with Him has helped me personally. In no way do I wish to offend anyone with what I write but conversely, I desire to bring to you some comfort. You may not be a Christian or perhaps you follow a different faith. I only know

Jesus as being real for me. This doesn't mean I understand why these things happen the way they do, but I trust in Him and his sovereignty and that He has a plan. What I am talking about is HOPE.

Before Joe died, I had some tough conversations with him as he had slowly come to terms with the fact he was going to die. One question was "what did I do to deserve this?" and another question was "what's going to happen to me when I die?" Both these questions were from his heart and questions I guess many people ask when their life is ending. The first question was easy to answer, absolutely nothing! Joe did nothing to deserve his illness and suffering, of course he didn't deserve this, and I think his real question was why me? And if you have read about the scandal above you will know, like in many other terrible situations, people do terrible things to other human beings. People cause suffering to other people.

In the next chapter I talk a little about Joe and his beliefs which came up in the middle of a heated debate we had had on terrorism. This debate had taken place some years earlier. But right now his question around death and eternity was far more relevant and significant than ever before. Through breaking voices and real sadness, we spoke of hope, about the Christian hope. This hope is a confident expectation of eternal life and eternal glory. I believe this was Joe's expectation. I believe Joe is in heaven right now.

After an arduous 4 decades of campaigning, the government recently announced that thousands of victims of the infected blood scandal will each receive a £100,000 interim compensation payment (for their lives). This currently is only for spouses and does not include parents or children of victims. A few months earlier the former Prime Minister John Major had the audacity to describe their plight this way; "what had happened to them was incredibly bad luck". Rightly, Kit Malthouse MP commented, "money will never compensate". Today, those infected continue to die at the rate of 1 person every 4 days.

Chapter 11 – Terror and the Worst Year

Towards the end of 2010 my wife Debbie and I were at a friend's house for a small party gathering. I had felt so fatigued for the entire past year, but now I could barely function. I recall saying to Debbie that if I didn't sit down now, I was going to fall to the floor. I was exhausted. At the back of my mind was this persisting thought; was I experiencing the spread of cancer having had two surgeries the year before on my right thigh for a malignant melanoma? What was to be a revelation to me and had struck me for the first time was when Debbie replied, "You have been like this since you went to that murder". The year 2009 to 2010 was the worst year of my life and career for many reasons.

For months I had noticed a mole on my right outer thigh that had changed shape. It had a small black patch on one edge that wasn't really much bigger that a tealeaf. I kept saying to myself I should make an appointment to see my doctor and have it checked, but like too many other people I kept procrastinating. Eventually I went to my GP who made a referral to dermatology. Six weeks later I walked into the dermatology department wearing my ambulance uniform as I was on duty that morning. Within half an hour I had 12 stitches as it was highly likely a malignant melanoma. A few more weeks later and I was back in hospital, this time for a re-excision, removing the first scar and taking a wide and deep margin of flesh. I was monitored closely for the next five years. The mole had been in a downward growth phase and had a Breslow thickness of 1.2mm, the depth measured from the skin to the deepest part of the tumour.

My longstanding crew mate and friend Chris 'Simbo' had retired a couple of years earlier, after serving 27 years on the front line as an ambulance technician. We stayed in regular contact with each other and Simbo would call me every weekend as soon as Country File had ended. He was concerned about my malignant mole diagnosis. I learned about his deep depression only two weeks before his death. I won't disclose any more information here other than this wonderful man chose to end his own life this same year. I hadn't cried like I did over his death since I had been a child. He left everyone who knew him stunned and grieving.

What came next was the worst incident of my entire career, a so called 'honour killing'.

Honour based violence is a practice used to control behaviour within families in order to protect perceived cultural and religious beliefs and honour. Violence can occur when perpetrators believe that a relative has shamed the family or the community by breaking their honour code.

Pause for thought: People do bad things to other people

We were nearing the end of a 12-hour shift and were sitting comfortably in the crew room. As is often the case, the shift to this point had been unremarkable and we were chatting and having a cup of tea. The time had just turned 19:06 hours when we were passed details of a serious assault, a female with significant arm injuries. The distance to the address was just 1.7 miles from the ambulance station and this didn't give us much time to take in all the details, but we were told a female had been assaulted with a machete type weapon. Thames Valley Police were on scene, so it was safe for us to approach and the assailant was already detained. Pete Howarth was driving and I was attending, and we were being backed up by little Daz who was on an RRV. The time to being on scene was just 6 minutes. We didn't have time to gather our thoughts or begin to worry about what might await us.

I grabbed as much equipment as I could carry and Pete and Daz brought everything else with them, following closely behind. As I hurried along the driveway, I was very aware of the large Police presence and saw to my right a young stocky male detained in hand cuffs. Police officers directed me to an upstairs bedroom as my crewmates followed. I went into the front bedroom and saw another young male lying by the entrance to the en-suite bathroom, apparently unconscious but without any visible injuries. Daz attended him as I entered the dimly lit dark bathroom. There was shattered glass everywhere from the shower screen door covering the entire floor and the bathroom suite was also smashed into pieces. What on earth had gone on here I briefly thought to myself as I muttered words of disbelief under my breath. It was a horror scene.

This lady was lying on her back with rapidly fading signs of life. As I placed an oxygen mask over her head, I felt my fingers slide into the deep lacerations in the back of her head and skull. I had never seen such a large quantity of blood, so much of it I was struggling not to slip over. One of her arms was amputated and the other was barely recognisable as an arm, having multiple pieces gouged out. Someone, *her own son*, had tried to behead her.

We were on scene for just 13 minutes and in hospital by 19:30 hours. Before Daz could close the rear ambulance doors I had intubated her. Pete and I stayed in the back as Daz drove as fast as he could to hospital. As we pulled away this poor lady went in cardiac arrest and despite significant attempts to restore her life both en-route and in hospital, she had sadly died. She had exsanguinated (completely bled out).

Later, that evening several things struck me that will never leave my memory. The ambulance and resuscitation room were cordoned off with police blue tape as part of the crime scene. All three of us had our clothes, ID badges and boots taken for forensic examination following serious crime procedure. As Pete removed his green uniform shirt, the vivid and stark image of him standing in the resuscitation room with his blood-soaked body caused complete silence. Both Daz and I, when lifting the patient had cut our fingertips from all the shower glass and we were required to give our own blood, in case of infection and cross contamination. We were all in deep shock.

A week or so later we all attended a hospital debrief which was also attended by the mortuary staff and emergency room staff. Everyone had opportunity to recall their part and express their feelings. The mortuary coroner recounted how in her mind this woman had fled for her life in fear, evidenced by her urinary incontinence during the assault. Mortuary staff stopped counting her injuries when they had reached 200.

Over the next year Daz, Pete and I had asked for counselling support on many occasions. I have to say we were badly let down. Our senior manager at that time just didn't get it. On the night of the murder he refused to attend the hospital or check our welfare because he was out food shopping. When I saw him a few days later he even commented that he knew we would be alright; a wild assumption. Over the passing year my mental health declined, until I sought professional help for myself. What surprised me was that I hadn't recognised the cause of my mental decline for myself even though I was trained to look out for these signs in other people. The ambulance service has got better at looking after its staff's health and wellbeing since then, but I feel there is still a great deal of room for improvement.

[1] Certain aspects of a traumatic event can have a significant impact upon the individual's mental health. How an event effects an individual depends on many factors including the event, the characteristics of the individual, the meaning of the trauma, social support, individual health and exposure to other stressors. My reaction to this event was a combination of emotions constituting of *threat, horror and loss*. People traumatised by an event often experience a pervasive sense of loss, including a loss of feeling safe, identity, control, trust, hope, loss of a person, personal belongings, self-worth, and so on. Such events may have been perceived as threatening our own life or the very essence of our self-worth and individuality thereby challenging strongly held beliefs.

These are our core beliefs. Such events are often shocking and abhorrent, causing horror and disgust. Events involving death or serious injury and where there is a feeling of wanting to have done more are likely to result in a greater impact upon the individual's mental health.

Terror attacks in France and so-called honour killings:

Pause for thought:

We fight and kill each other
In your name defending You
Oh, the free will You have given we have made a mockery of.
Dolly Parton – Hello God

On Sunday afternoon after lunch I met with a group of friends for a band rehearsal. The band consists of five guys from different backgrounds and beliefs, two of whom I would say are un-churched Christians, one atheist and Joe, my closest friend of more than 35 years. Joe and I have been through many life trials together, been best man to one another and shared our deepest thoughts and emotions. Joe has his own set of beliefs and would maybe loosely call himself Christian but recognised the value in *all* faiths and *all* people. Without hesitation I can say I do not believe that we could ever really fall out, regardless of the disagreements we sometimes have.

During a coffee break the recent terror attacks in France came up in conversation and what followed was a rather heated variance of opinion. I must admit I was already feeling on edge because I had not found much spare time recently to practice and came to the rehearsal studio feeling very tense and het up. Even so, without excuse my response was quite stark and I remember feeling embarrassed at what I had said.

I announced that I hated Islam and that it was founded on evil. Although embarrassed by this statement, recognising my hatred as prejudiced hostility, I felt there was some justification to what I had said. At this point Joe was defensive of the individual Muslim and Islam and this only seemed to add to my annoyance, and I felt I needed to say more to 'prove' my argument. The other band members were slightly bemused by our heated debate.

At that time I had felt overwhelmed and indignant by the constant news reports both globally and locally around acts of terror, so called honour killings, grooming of young girls and sexual exploitation, beheadings, inequality of Muslim women, extremist views and Jihad all from within puritanical and radical Islam. My frustration had spilled over. We continued our rehearsal, agreeing to disagree about our views. As we continued, I felt distracted by my earlier feelings, aware that I had become quite upset. Ultimately, I suppose I felt a sense of helplessness and weariness for the future.

Many reasons could be given for my outburst and intense emotional state, but this would only hide the reality behind my perspective. In truth I agree with Joe's points of view, but my own view was tainted by personal experience. You have read above about the so-called honour killing I attended in 2010 which took me to an emotional place I cannot begin to put into words. Since that time, I have come to recognise that my struggle was with the people who distort and malign Islam, not Islam itself.

Religious and violent extremism

It is evident that religious and violent extremism is at the heart of much of what has been said so far. For millennia violence carried out in the name of God has been a common theme in *all* religions. Even the Jewish Zealots carried out terror attacks against the Roman Empire in the first century. Many people today are being coerced or are deluded in their thinking that terror and violence is God's calling on their life. As I try to understand my own abhorrence to such ideology, I am reminded that the salvation Jesus has offered me has come from His suffering, servitude and vulnerability. God does not ask me to shed my blood for Him; the exact opposite is true; He has shed His blood for me and laid down His life. This is love.

As I think about all this prayerfully, I am reminded that we are all made in God's own image and likeness. This infinite value of _every_ human being stands in opposition to violence. Jesus has challenged us to love our enemies and this is where the battle ground begins for many Christians. As Christians we are also called to overcome evil with good. 'The fruit of the Spirit is love, joy peace, patience, kindness, goodness, faithfulness, gentleness and self-control' (Gal.5:22), these are the antithesis of violent hatred; the overwhelming Christian ethos is love. Love in the bible is extreme and even scandalous as one minister recently described it.

On love Jesus proclaimed that loving our neighbour followed loving God. Here however I believe is the salient point, to love in this way requires humility. Humility as a virtue is a major theme throughout scripture and from it love, peace and harmony with all people emanates. It is humility that allows us to see the dignity and value of all humankind and affirms our inherent worth. It is through being humble that anger, hatred and prejudice can be dissipated. What greater example of humility we have is that the author of life should be nailed to a wooden stake? Through being humble we acknowledge God's way (Psalm25:9).

'The Lord lifts up the humble, he casts the wicked to the ground' (Psalm 147:6). None of the wicked in the end shall escape God's justice. Being humble toward others does not imply that criminals act with impunity. The Bible firmly supports civil governments but ultimately all judgment is reserved for God. As Christians we are challenged to examine ourselves and to humble ourselves. As I share these sentiments of course I recognise that most people from all faiths share these same truths. I recognise within Islam there is also love and holiness. This is not a polemic on Islam but a candid reflection on my own personal struggles to enable change.

So, what about God's **Justice**?

Pause for thought: Ponder this question. Do I enjoy having free will; a choice to choose for myself?

That adage what goes round comes round often remains unfulfilled in this life, doesn't it? We want *justice* but it just doesn't happen for many of us. So, we either blame God or we simply just don't believe he exists at all.

People often complain about God allowing bad things to happen. They level this question, why doesn't He do something about it? But we should also ask ourselves this question; do we really want God to step into our violent societies with its wickedness, debauchery and immoral behaviour with His justice? [2]Brendon Hatmaker in his book Barefoot Church muses "Sometimes I'd like to ask God why he allows poverty, famine & injustice when he could do something about it. But I'm afraid God might ask me the same question. "

I believe people blame God for the choices He allows us to make (free will), but they do not necessarily want to take responsibility for their own wrong choices. They want God to fix this broken world, but they do not want Him to fix them. To have the choice to be good, we must have the choice to do the opposite; otherwise there is no choice at all. This implies we want evil removed from the world without removing evil itself. People want God to remove the painful results of choices without restriction on our own choices. Justice comes at a price. Can you pay the price of justice for your own failings? We certainly cannot measure up to God's absolute righteousness.

So often, when choosing between good and bad, what we are doing is making moral choices. This further argues for the existence of God because we intrinsically know what is good and bad. Atheism has no basis for morality because our choices without God would just be arbitrary. If you want to understand this point further please read Appendix 1, Science and Religion which goes into detail about this subject.

Chapter 12 Corona King Arthur Last Year and Hope

A corona is part of a body that resembles a crown. The Covid-19 virus is an abbreviation of **Co**rona **vi**rus **d**isease 20**19**, the word Corona comes from the Latin for crown and the virus was so called because of its spherical shape and its club like spikes. The first confirmed Coved-19 patient I attended was on 14th March 2020. We were asked to attend a 43-year-old female, who reported a continuous cough, severe fatigue, shortness of breath and was very scared. Early in the pandemic we were issued with FFP3 masks recommended by WHO, for the outbreak of SARS. These were soon removed from ambulances due to being costly, and replaced with the less expensive fluid repellent FFP2 masks. As we put on our level 2 PPE in the back of the ambulance, I remember feeling very nervous. The UK was in lockdown, this was an unknown and uncertain time for everybody and there was a real fear of catching this potentially deadly virus.

Boris Johnson had announced the UK's first National lockdown on 23rd March 2020 and Emily our youngest daughter was already 7 months pregnant. We were all really worried as there was widespread concern about Covid-19 disease and harm to expectant mothers and their unborn child. To our absolute delight, Arthur was born on 19.05.20 at 0307am weighing 6Ib 10 oz. He is an absolute blessing in a time that was filled with worry and uncertainty. Because Arthur was our first grandchild and bearing such a celebrated and iconic name, we often call him King Arthur. He is awesome. I will never forget the moment I set eyes on him in his mother's arms looking through the glass of the maternity delivery suite doors. We weren't allowed in to see Arthur directly due to Covid rules, but what staggered me the most is hard to describe. His mum Emily's countenance was changed to that of someone with complete fulfilment and sheer joy.

As the virus spread and gripped the whole country, new information came out of London hospitals and the London ambulance service. A drop in Oxygen saturations on exertion was deemed significant. During the first wave we had been strongly encouraged to discharge patients on scene. This felt wrong on every level and went against all previous experience. If a Covid patient was taken to the ED, they were often rapidly discharged. We also left a lot of people at home who would have normally been taken to hospital. Crews were able to access a helpline manned by a consultant for advice and support and invariably we were advised to discharge on scene giving worsening advice. Many patients appeared well enough early on, but typically at around day 10 after contracting the virus, their illness could significantly worsen. During this first lockdown the accident and emergency departments were almost completely deserted and nearly every call to the ambulance service was for Covid-19. It was as if all the other illnesses and incidents had ceased.

Lateral flow testing allows us to identify individuals who are asymptomatic carriers of COVID-19 and isolate them quickly. It gives a result which is valid for the specific time and date the test is taken only – therefore when you return a negative result this is only valid at that exact time. It does not mean that you are negative a few hours later – or the next day, as you may have, unknowingly, had contact with the virus and become infected.

The first time I was tested for Covid-19 during the pandemic was on 05.12.20 with SARS-Cov-2 Antigen Rapid Qualitative home test kit. This was 7 months after the first lockdown. During this time, I worked every day on the front line. The government then announced that the Pfizer/Biotech vaccine was to be rolled out from 08.12.20 for the over 80's, for key workers, NHS frontline staff and care workers. The earliest I could get vaccinated was 21.01.21 in Milton Keynes.

We transported one patient who was in his 40's into Milton Keynes general hospital. We couldn't get his oxygen saturations above 84% even with 15 litres of Oxygen via a non-re-breather mask. He was kept in the back of our ambulance for an hour outside the hospital because there wasn't any room inside for him in the designated Covid-19 red area. He was terrified and said to me he believed he would never go home again. I reassured him but in the back of my mind I knew he was probably right. This was the reality of Covid-19 infection.

If any anti-vaxxers out there have doubt, in the 23 years I have been in the ambulance service I have never seen such desperately sick people, unable to breathe and with abject fear as their companion. Many ill-informed people who had earlier refused the vaccine sat in the back of my ambulance on high flow Oxygen, articulating their regret at not being vaccinated, with a real fear that they were going to die. Many did.

As we started the New Year in 2021 further lockdown restrictions were introduced across the UK. Work colleague and close friend Mark Greenhill had been admitted to the Covid ward at Stoke Mandeville hospital as 1325 new deaths in one day were reported bringing the death toll to 79,833. On the 8th January (2021) 31,624 people were currently being treated in UK hospitals and it was estimated that 1 person in 50 have the virus. This period was very scary. Mark, after many months of convalescence, returned to work in good health, thank God.

This year had been incredibly difficult and presented the following challenges for me:

My dearest friend of 40+ years Joe, spoken about many times in this book died on 10th July 2021 after a brave battle with cancer as a direct result of the biggest scandal the NHS has ever seen (see chapter 10). He was the most talented, irrepressible powerhouse of a man I ever met, and his death has left a huge hole is so many lives.

I finished late on 68 shifts out of 142 long shifts. Late meals or no meal break at all totalled 43 often coinciding on the same days as the late finishes.

I caught Covid-19 the day after I went on annual leave on 04.08.21.

I hurt my back lifting a man who weighed in excess of 38 stone.

[1]Research carried out by the University Of Manchester Institute Of Science and Technology into stress factors in a range of occupations scored the Ambulance Service at **6.3** with 10 being the highest level. Out of the 50 occupations being researched the average score was **4.9** which put the ambulance service high on the scale of stressful occupations.

The Independent Newspaper published an article by the Health Care Commission reporting that **34%** of ambulance staff suffered from work related stress. It also reported that an assessment of *Oxfordshire* ambulance service staff carried out in 1999 estimated that **20%** of its employees were suffering from Post-Traumatic Stress Disorder, now believed to be much higher with the increase in demand on the Ambulance Service.

[3]A recent UK Government document on Health at work and sickness absence, reported the public sector continues to have rising levels of work-related stress. Within the NHS it is Ambulance personnel that have the highest sickness absence rate of *all* NHS workers. Ambulance staff scored 6.21 per cent on this survey compared to nurses who had the lowest rate of just 1.05 per cent.

During the last few years, I have become increasingly restless, feeling exhausted physically and emotionally and feeling more and more overwhelmed by my role as a paramedic. I was becoming very aware that I was beginning to feel increasingly *broken*. A buzz word was being thrown around describing this broken feeling as "compassion fatigue" where you have very little empathy left to give. While this does seem to be true for some people in the ambulance service, I would describe my own situation as feeling the weight of too much responsibility and wanting to relinquish that responsibility – for me this was occupational burnout. I would often find myself saying "I can't face another traumatic death or another cardiac arrest or sick child". I couldn't continue to face dressing in level 3 PPE any longer. I didn't anymore want to be the person racing against time and chaos, fighting to resuscitate the life of another human being, responsible for their life in my hands. Other reasons for these feeling are multifaceted:

The role of paramedic has evolved over the years and now the national requirement is primarily a degree in paramedic science. I have seen many changes during this time such as access to many more drugs, the introduction of rapid response vehicles, the development of new skills such as Intraosseous infusion (IO) where drugs are given directly into the marrow of the bone, greater technology, better safeguarding, alternate care pathways, higher clinical standards and better infection control.

The demand on the Ambulance service and hospitals has increased yearly and over my last year it was at the highest I had ever seen. Ambulance crews have been unable to hand patients over to hospital care because of bed blocking. As many as 15 patients have been waiting in the corridor on stretchers and several more patients kept on the ambulance vehicles until spaces become available. Some crews have been tasked to care for other crew's patients, often looking after 5 patients at a time. This process is known as Hospital Ambulance Liaison Officer (HALO) due to the pressures in hospital. Members of the public are regularly waiting more than 4 hours for an ambulance to arrive at their address, or worse, outside in the street. Single responders on cars are waiting long periods for a double manned crew to back them up causing huge amounts of stress to everyone concerned and putting lives at risk.

Ambulance crews working 12-hour shifts are regularly going 9 or more hours without any breaks. The shift patterns are antisocial, have no structure and include ridiculous finishing times such as 3.00am. Staff work most weekends, are severely fatigued and morale is at an all-time low. The past few months had seen a huge exit of staff while many more are actively seeking new employment. Sickness levels remain at a record high. In response South Central Ambulance Service is recruiting overseas to help meet the current shortfall of 120 paramedics, looking primarily to Australia. In September 2021 Health Education England (HEE) launched a Global Paramedic Recruitment pilot aiming to address a national shortage of paramedics. It is anticipated that 48 paramedics will arrive to start induction training in late 2022.

Being human, fatigued and apathetic, employees are finding ways to compensate. They are taking breaks in patient's homes, having a drink when offered and taking time when completing paperwork. Crews time their arrival at the Emergency Department to meet the end of their shift to ensure that they are not going to be passed another job. Many are on long term sick leave because of stress. All these factors raise serious questions and add to the existing demand problems.

All this raises a serious question. Is it ethical to try and get some down time looking after one's own needs? How much of this responsibility lies with the individual clinician and how much rests on the organisation as it fails to meet its staff's basic human needs?

Pause for thought: Being religious isn't the same thing as faith, but faith may lead to something of religion.

Personal and Social Ethics

Scripture teaches us that we have a moral duty before God. Some people believe that being moral is a choice. Many other people believe that simply by leading a good life and by doing good deeds there is a guaranteed afterlife in heaven. This is not the mainstream Christian belief, where salvation is by faith alone as an act of God's grace. Some denominations of Christianity teach that we must add good works to grace in order to receive merit for salvation, while others insist there is no need for good works at all. Whereas faith should produce good deeds in the believer, if you are paid for what you do have you not received your reward? If we seek to better the welfare of others because it makes us feel good is this act ultimately motivated by self-interest?

In the wider sense throughout scripture rewards and punishments are associated with both moral duty and self-interest. For example, it benefits me to have faith because by it I receive salvation. This is putting your own needs first in a sense. 2 Corinthians 5:10 tells us that recompense will be made by Christ himself for the deeds we have done in this life, good or bad. I feel that scripture tells us that it is the motivation behind the act that makes all the difference. We are taught that it is better to give than receive, and through faith we operate in this sphere, by faith delighting in God's will and purpose. This is our motivation.

I believe that as long as our intent is to live our life in a way that is pleasing to God our career choice is incidental. Scripture reminds us to commit our work to God and to acknowledge him in all that we do. The question of when it is right to put yourself before others appears to be ambiguous with some scripture, but if our intent is right this does not come into conflict with God's word. The Holy Spirit reminds us that our body is a temple in which He indwells and should be glorified with good health. There are occasions when it is perfectly good and ethical to meet your own needs ahead of others. We each need to examine our own hearts and motive to know when this is right. I believe we do not do good works to get to heaven, but as a result of being saved and to verify our faith good works result.

It is with sadness that I feel the front-line ambulance service is no longer a career for life for many people. This does not mean I wouldn't recommend it as a career opportunity for anyone who wants to become a paramedic. It has been an incredible journey for me and most of my experiences I will cherish. If you join the ambulance service, you will save and impact many lives. However, today the role is incredibly demanding.

The modern paramedic will have undertaken a university degree and has many career opportunities to follow if they desire a change in direction. Many paramedics go on to work in GP practices; some go offshore to work on oil rigs. There is work in hospitals in accident and emergency or perhaps you might want to be a medic on film sets? Some go into training school to teach or lecture at university. You could train further to become a specialist paramedic or work in critical care. There are also many opportunities for promotion. The options are many so if it is your heart's desire follow it, you will touch the hem of death and sometimes defeat it, and you will certainly touch lives in the here and now. You will make a difference to your community. You will be a part of a team where the camaraderie is strong, you will form close relationships and make friends for life. As a paramedic you will never stop learning and you will never have seen it all, every day is different and there is always excitement.

Leaving the ambulance service.

As 2021 ended and further scandal hit Downing Street over alleged 'breaking of the rules' amongst Tory MP's last Christmas, Omicron Covid variant was rapidly on the increase. The UK recorded the highest daily cases of Covid since the pandemic began at 78,610 infections (15.12.21). UK chief medical officers had increased their assessment of the Covid Omicron threat to level 4 and SAGE warned that the number of people requiring hospital care could be significant. Boris Johnson's authority had been challenged as Conservative backbenchers rejected plans for vaccination certificates. On the local news South Central Ambulance Service declared a major incident in Reading, Berkshire as a block of flats caught fire.

As I wrote this, I felt a mixture of emotions having offered my resignation from the ambulance service. My last shift was Wednesday 22nd December 2021, covering a 08:00am to 20:00 shift. My official last day was Tuesday 28th December 2021 having some time off over Christmas. As I said farewell to my colleagues who have been like family, I was also filled with excitement to start a new job as a 'Deputy Bereavement Listening Lead' at the Florence Nightingale Hospice.

Hope:

At whatever time you find yourself reading this book, I'm sure there continues to be major global issues such as famine, water scarcity, hunger, pollution, wars, disease, climate change other global issues and of course the need for an ambulance service. In this current dispensation of human Government and the rule of humankind all Governments will fail to make any real or lasting change. So are we without hope?

Without hope the meaning of life seems to have no real value, and is certainly fleeting. However, for the Christian believer there exists a 'confident expectation' of eternal glory and life after death. Only Jesus can bring true peace and prosperity to all nations and the whole earth, bringing rest to the animal kingdom and freeing us from death. At Jesus' return evil will be defeated and the earth will be restored.

May God bless each person who has taken time to read about my experiences and my thoughts about my career and God's plan for us all? I pray that in some way this book has blessed you and given you hope and time to *pause for thought* and consider your relationship with God.

Chapter 13 – Step into Eternity

Who qualifies for heaven and how do we get there?

"For the believer there is hope beyond the grave, because Jesus Christ has opened the door to heaven for us by His death and resurrection." Billy Graham.

Pause for thought: What we believe about life after death directly affects what we believe about life before death[1]

Frome despair to hope:

Hope is a state of anticipation for a better future. For the Christian believer hope is held with a confident expectation, an expectation of a life after this one. It is my sincere desire that you have been inspired to discover this hope for yourself. We all need hope because this world is broken. Peter the apostle wrote, because God raised Jesus from the dead your faith and hope can be confidently placed in Him (1 Peter 1:21). There is one, who adores you, place your trust in Him.

Martin Luther during the Reformation stated "Justification is by Faith alone"

- The object OF our Faith IS Jesus Christ.

The bible teaches that there is only one unpardonable sin, that is, *only* ONE unforgivable sin. It is the failure to believe in Jesus Christ as the very Son of God and that He purchased a **full** pardon for our sins on the cross.

It is called the blasphemy of the Holy Spirit (the unpardonable sin) and it is to reject the Holy Spirit's witness to Jesus Christ's offer of salvation. Jesus promised the disciples that He would send the Holy Spirit to empower them to proclaim the three most important truths of the gospel. Jesus said "when He comes (the Holy Spirit) He will convict the world of sin, and of righteousness, and of judgment: of sin, because they do not believe in Me; of righteousness, because I go to my Father and you see Me no more; of judgment, because the ruler of this world is judged." John 16:8-11

1. He will convict the world that they must believe in Jesus and His pardon of sin. To reject this pardon is the ONE sin Jesus cannot atone for. Jesus paid for every other sin that we might commit, but we can reject the free gift of salvation that He alone purchased with His blood and which cost the Father the death of His only son. To do so is to reject the pardon and our sins remain upon us. A pardon is not a pardon until it is personally received by Faith. To reject the convicting power of the Holy Spirit is to commit blasphemy against His witness.

2. The Holy Spirit will convict the world about the only righteousness God can accept: the righteousness of Jesus. We give Him our sin, and He gives us His righteousness in return. "For He made Him who knew no sin to be sin for us, that we might become the righteousness of God in Him" 2 Corinthians 5:21

3. The Holy Spirit convicts the world of the certainty of eternal judgment if they reject God's free salvation. "He who believes in Him is not condemned; but he who does not believe is condemned already, because he has not believed in the name of the only begotten Son of God" John 3:18

Can you be saved after death? The bible says;

"And inasmuch as it is appointed for men to die once and after this comes judgment, so Christ also, having been offered once to bear the sins of many...." Hebrews 9:27

When we die the opportunity to receive Christ is over, just as when Christ died on the cross our sins were once for all paid.

Jesus shouted out on the cross *"teteles'tai"* which means **PAID IN FULL.** His death was victorious. Jesus cried out, "It is finished."

"For by grace you have been saved through **Faith**, and that not of yourself, it is a gift of God, not of works, lest anyone should boast" Ephesians 2:8-9

When we die at that moment our soul and spirit go to be face to face with the Lord.

"…to be absent from the body, and present with the Lord" 2 Corinthians 5:8

Heaven

Where will you spend eternity when this life is over? That I believe is a choice. Heaven is a Kingdom, a celestial city, an eternal home, a real place and you can go there. Jesus said Heaven is His Father's house. There will be societies there, we will live in houses, and there will be banquets and feasts. You will have a real body in heaven that will be immortal. I believe there is a place beyond this world, a spiritual realm far more beautiful than we can imagine. A place is prepared there for you already because Jesus promised this to all His followers. Heaven is not a figment of the imagination; it is a prepared place just beyond the veil of this world. Right now, your redeemer is in Heaven. You cannot get to Heaven by any other means than by Him. There are not many ways into heaven, there is only one. Jesus said: "I am the way and the truth and the life. No one comes to the Father except through me - John 14:16. It only takes faith.

Now, this may come as a surprise, not only is Heaven our destination when we die but we are also to live in eternity on a new earth! How is this? Going to Heaven is only a temporary place on our journey. Ultimately, after Heaven we will in time live in a superior physical body on a perfect earth in a new creation. This is clear in scripture but is beyond the scope of this book. The point I hope you understand is that eternity will be beautiful and our enjoyment of it will be far greater than our imaginations can grasp, and we will be free from sickness, sorrow, suffering and death.

Now is the time that you can *step into eternity*. God wants to you to be saved and enter eternity with Him in this very moment. [2]Have you ever confided in a trusted friend or a family member and asked them to listen to your story? You spoke to them because they love you and you trusted them and didn't expect then to judge you. You wanted to be accepted and receive their grace and mercy for your situation, right?

Does your friend or relative have more grace, love and mercy than the creator God Himself who stepped into this life and died in your place? If you trust in Him and believe He died and rose again on the third day for your sins, declare He is your Lord and saviour and you will step into eternity. Anyone who accepts Jesus into their life is eligible for salvation. The bible says: "Believe in the Lord Jesus, and you will be saved" Acts 16:31. There is no other way because He is the only person who can atone for you. 1 John 5:11-12 says - And this is the testimony: God has given us eternal life, and this life is in his Son. [V12]Whoever has the Son has life; whoever does not have the Son of God does not have life.

If you believe that Jesus died for *you* then please say this prayer out loud and you will go to Heaven upon your death if you continue to trust Him. More importantly, your salvation is right now.

'Lord Father God,

[3]I come to you in the name of Jesus. Your word says that anyone who calls on the name of Jesus will be saved. Lord I repent of every one of my sins. Jesus, by faith I declare with my mouth you to be my personal Lord and saviour and believe that you died for me, being raised to life again on the third day. Thank you for forgiving my sins and giving me eternal life. Holy Spirit would you now fill me and dwell in my heart always. In the name of the Father, Son and Holy Spirit, Amen'.

Now that you have confessed Jesus as Lord and received His free gift go out and tell someone. And if you are able, go find other Christians in your area to build each other's faith and share fellowship with one another. You are now a child of God. If you said this prayer, right now the angels in Heaven are celebrating. Jesus said, "I tell you, there is rejoicing in the presence of the angels of God over one sinner who repents" (Luke 15:10).

Science and religion are often depicted as diametrically opposed disciplines. The relationship between these two areas of knowledge has been turbulent and confusing. Today, for many people, living with a modern scientific world view, the primary issue regarding religious belief and science is which of these two systems of knowledge is the most rational way to explain human life and the universe in which we live. Can the relationship between science and religion be characterised by conflict or concord? This brief work will summarise how I feel that not only are science and religion agreeable, but how they can underpin one other.

The ethologist and evolutionary biologist Professor Richard Dawkins popularised the notion that only modern science can answer the origins of the universe and life. Atheist Dawkins' antireligious assertion is that religious faith is a delusion (Dawkins, 2006, 28). In a lecture given by Dawkins he does however view religion as a scientific theory (1994), seeing science and religion as rival explanations for our existence and as conflicting theories. Dawkins in his lecture identifies a profound mystery in science which has not yet been fully understood. Many Christian scientists, such as physician-geneticist Francis Collins see no conflict between science and faith, insisting that '...They coexist. They illuminate each other'. For Collins, this profound mystery in science is the revelation of a supernatural God (2000). Similarly, modern astronomer and discoverer of quasars Allan Sandage said, 'God to me is a mystery but is the explanation for the miracle of existence' (New York Times, 2015).

New atheists are offering science without religion as their default position, asserting that science in fact should replace religion and God altogether (New Scientist, 2006, 8-11). Geisler points out that while it is true science is based on empirical methods, science does not disprove the existence of God, but shares a common search to understand reality, the universe and the human person. Geisler points out that there are limits to what science can observe and quantify (2012, 525). Lennox rightly argues that the natural sciences have helped us to better understand the universe in which we live, unveiling and verifying its inherent order and intelligibility (2011, 47).

History acknowledges that biblical interpretation used by the Reformers had given rise to much great scientific advancement, as they felt able to challenge the hegemony of the Roman Catholic Church theologians (Eiseley, 1969, 62). Nicolaus Copernicus, a devout Christian astronomer, controversially challenging the Roman Catholic Church's beliefs, published an anonymous work claiming that the sun, not the earth, was at the centre of our solar system (BBC, 2014). His work was later supported by Galileo Galilei, the Italian astronomer and mathematician, when he built telescopes and began looking through them at the heavens. Galilei's own studies confirmed the Copernican heliocentric theory (sun-centred) view of our solar system. Galilei in 1615 wrote, 'God is known by nature in his works, and by doctrine in his revealed word' (Galli and Olsen 2000, 355). Fee and Stuart rightly comment that many have had a theological bias, failing to recognise the human as well as the divine character of scripture. The Bible was not wrong; it was the interpretation of it that was wrong (2002, 13-19).

Looking to explain existence and understanding of the universe, some particle physicists hold to the hypothetical theory that the universe had developed randomly, known as the theory of everything (ToE). Physicist and cosmologist Stephen Hawking asserts that the laws of physics will eventually explain such origins of the universe, these self-perpetuating laws are used to theorise the big bang theory (2010, 180). I believe that Lennox is right when he observes that this notion assumes that God was not the cause of the big bang or such laws (2011, 31). On this subject of a random universe, theologian Ward (n.d.) argues that blind chance and random development leading to a complex contingent universe is infinitely impossible without God. Ward does allow for what he calls 'indeterminacy', that is, the way things are allows for moral freedom to evolve, given ordering by a rational, wise and powerful God who acts within his creation (volume 11, 13).

Barbour, a Professor of both physics and religion, in his dialogical approach toward science and theology, observes that the scientific understanding of the world we see around us influences our moral choices. Morality itself is a field of scientific study, as are social sciences such as psychology and anthropology, seeking answers about human behaviour, motives and actions (1989-91). Van Til (Min 2009, 74) asks the pertinent question, what is the motive, the standard and purpose of human action? Because science alone cannot tell us what is right and wrong, Craig (Strobel 2000, 79-81) rightly argues that if morality is only a by-product of socio-biological evolution then individual ethics is arbitrary, and there can be no absolute right or wrong. Theological inquiry into ethics seeks to set principles for acting rightly based upon the highest good defined by scripture (Grenz, Guretzki & Nording, 1999, 47). To demonstrate this point graphically, can you discuss therapeutic abortion and foetal pain without reference to some ethical framework? I believe an answer without God is subjective depending whether you believe that inflicting pain on a foetus is somehow wrong (Bognar, Hirose, 2104, 19).

Seeking a bridge between science, cosmology and theology to explain human life and the universe in which we live, a unifying theory is found in the anthropic principle. This notion explains Geisler (2012, 22), reasons that everything in the universe has been solely tailored for humankind. Life appears to be deliberate, somehow actually required by the universe. Agnostic astronomer Jastrow concedes that every physical parameter from cosmic size and distance to subatomic particles from the moment of the big bang is the remarkable fine-tuning necessary for man to live in (1982, 17). Many in the scientific community find the teleological argument for God's existence is strengthened by the anthropic principle. Philosopher of science Stephen Meyer asserts that modern sciences such as cosmology and physics are unveiling 'intelligent design' by a pre-existent intelligence; saying a theistic designer is the most plausible explanation (Behe, Dembski and Meyer 2000. 56-57, 63).

Science and religion do not need to be rival explanations for existence but can engage with each other having equal value to help us understand the world in which we live. Theologians seeking the mystery of God find revelation in the physical universe, the sciences often providing a greater knowledge, helping shape theological understanding. Religion can offer sapience to scientists who engage with issues of ethical concern.

B: DRIVING TRAINING PROGRAMME I
B:1 DRIVING
B1:1 AMBULANCE DRIVING AND THE HIGHWAY CODE
(including Road Traffic Law)
The student should be able to:

Describe the importance of the Highway Code to drivers of the ambulance service.

Drive in accordance with the Highway Code in various situations encountered.

State the basic responsibility of the ambulance service. Identify a selection of road traffic signs.

Explain the duties of the driver in the conveyance of patients.

Drive an ambulance with consideration of the conditions, comfort and safety of the patient.

State what exemptions from normal traffic regulations ambulance vehicles have on an emergency.

Key Learning Points
Supporting evidence is required of the student's understanding of:

- The highway code and how to apply it
- The service's responsibility for patient conveyance
- How the patient's condition governs a journey
- The driver's responsibilities
- How the driver's responsibilities should be carried out during a journey
- Why complete concentration and careful driving are so vital
- The importance of smooth use of gears and foot controls (co-ordination)
- Compliance with Road Traffic Regulations and the Highway Code
- What is meant by the term 'exemption' and how it affects ambulance drivers.

B1:2 VEHICLE DAILY INSPECTION
The student should be able to:
Demonstrate a vehicle daily inspection. Demonstrate a driver's daily cab inspection.

Key Learning Points
Supporting evidence is required of the student's understanding of:

- The items to check daily
- The reasons for carrying out a vehicle daily inspection
- The check list for the driver's cab
- The reasons for a cockpit drill.

B1:3 DRIVING PLANS AND THE SYSTEM OF VEHICLE CONTROL
The student should be able to:

Describe the basis of a driving plan.
Make and carry out driving decisions, without hesitation, in a methodical manner. Discuss the importance of observation.
Whilst driving give a basic commentary to demonstrate observation and assessment of road signs and hazards.
Describe and demonstrate the three main features of the revised system of vehicle control (position, speed and gear).

Key Learning Points
Supporting evidence is required of the student's understanding of:
- What is meant by a 'driving plan'
- What is meant by 'concentration'
- Why some drivers fail to make a driving plan
- What factors are taken into consideration when formulating a driving plan
- Why observation is important
- How to link observation to potential hazards
- That you should consider every possibility, including mistakes by other drivers
- Why recognition and observance of road markings and road traffic signs is important
- Why the System of Vehicle Control was devised?
- The three main features of the revised system
- Their correct sequence
- Why you should follow them closely
- The term 'Hazard' and the three main types
- Applying the modified 'system' when making manoeuvres

B1:4 ACCELERATION
The student should be able to:
Demonstrate good acceleration technique.
Demonstrate the procedures to achieve the highest standards of acceleration.

Answer several relevant questions.

The key learning points
Supporting evidence is required of the students understanding of:
- The meaning of 'acceleration' sense
- Why good forward observation is important
- How the characteristics of a vehicle affects its acceleration
- The definition of "acceleration sense"
- How to maintain speed on a curve
- The road condition which need extra thought when accelerating
- How to make use of 'engine breaking'
- The correct way to move off in an automatic vehicle

B1:5 BREAKING
The student should be able to;
Skilfully apply the brakes to achieve optimum patient care.
Demonstrate good breaking techniques for smoothness and patient comfort.
Answer several relevant questions.

Key learning points
Supporting evidence is required of the students understanding of:
- The rules of breaking
- Why using brakes skilfully is important
- When to slow down by easing pressure on the accelerator
- When you need to use the brake pedal
- What 'three pressure tapering braking' is and how to apply it
- The factors you need to take into consideration, whatever method of slowing down you use.

B1:6 STEERING
The student should be able to:
Demonstrate the correct way to hold and turn the steering wheel.
Using the steering technique to steer a vehicle through a set obstacle course using both forward and reverse gears.
Answer a number of relevant questions.

Key learning points
Supporting evidence is required of the students understanding of:

- The correct way to hold and manipulate the steering wheel
- The reasons for doing things this way
- The rules for steering
- The factors taken into consideration to give optimum control.

B1:7 REVERSING
The student should be able to:
Describe the principles of safe reversing.
Describe the areas where reversing is dangerous.
Reverse and manoeuvre a vehicle through a set obstacle course.

Key learning points
Supporting evidence is required of the students understanding of:
- When and why many accidents happen with ambulances
- The safe procedure for reversing an ambulance
- The importance or correct positioning of the vehicle at the start of the manoeuvre
- The importance of setting driving mirrors
- The tighter the manoeuvre the slower the speed.

- Why the use of gears is such an important driving skill
- The aspects of driving which lead to effective use of a manual gearbox
- What your aims should be in your use of the gears
- The importance of co-ordination clutch and accelerator

B1:8 MANUAL GEARBOX
The student should be able to;
Demonstrate good gear changing and discuss why it is important.
Discuss the main principles of good gear changing.

B1:9 SKIDS
The student should be able to:
State the definition of skids.
Describe the factors to minimise the risk of skidding.
Answers several relevant questions and on a skid training facility, recognise and correct the three types of skid.

Key learning points
Supporting evidence is required of the students understanding of:

118

- What a skid is and what features of the tyres may be involved
  - What diving actions cause a skid
  - The road conditions which can present skid hazards
  - How to drive to avoid skids
  - Where counteracting skids can be practised
  - What cadence braking is
  -

B1:10 AUTOMATIC GEARBOX *(optional)*
The student should be able to:
List the two types of automatic gearboxes sued in ambulance vehicles.
Demonstrate the principles for safe and smooth use.
State how to avoid bad habits and faults.
Demonstrate selection and use of the various gears.

Key learning points
Supporting evidence is required of the students understanding of:
- The types of automatic gearboxes used in the ambulance service
- The various positions for each gearbox and how to engage them
- The correct sequence for starting and normal driving with the gearbox
- What is acceptable to I or L
- Factors to bear in mind when starting an automatic transmission vehicle
- Why you should never park in P without applying the handbrake as well
- What kick-down is and at which speeds you would use it
- The common driving faults to avoid
-

C: ADVANCED DRIVING PROGRAMME II
C:1 EMERGENCY DRIVING
C1:1 ROAD TRAFFIC LAW

The student should be able to:
State what exemptions from normal traffic regulations ambulance vehicles have on an emergency.
State when and how these exemptions can be used.
Describe the procedure if you have an accident.
Discuss the guidelines on legal matters involving accidents.
Drive in compliance with the current Road Traffic Law.

Key learning points

Supporting evidence is required of the students understanding of:
- Compliance with Road Traffic Law Regulations and the Highway Code
- What is meant by the term 'exemption' and how it affects ambulance drivers
- Lighting regulations as applied to an ambulance
- The rules about seatbelts
- Construction and use as applied to an ambulance
- What actions to take if involved in a road traffic accident
- Who owns your ambulance and what effect that has on insurance
- What to do if you are prosecuted for a motoring offence
- How 'standard of care' and 'negligence' are defined in civil law.

C1:2 THE SYSTEM OF VEHICLE CONTROL

The student should be able to:

Describe and demonstrate he six features of vehicle control.

Key learning points

Supporting evidence is required of the students understanding of:
- Why the system of vehicle control was devised
- The six features of the system
- Their correct sequence
- Why you should follow them closely
- The importance of using the latest edition of Roadcraft
- The term "Hazard" and the three main types
- Applying the 2system" when making manoeuvres
- Early commencement of the system.
-

C1:3 SPEED AND SAFETY

The student should be able to:

State the principles affecting how speed is experienced.

Describe the guidelines for choosing the appropriate speed.

Drive at a safe speed for ant situation encountered.

Key learning points

Supporting evidence is required of the students understanding of:
- The conditions which determine the speed at which a vehicle should be driven
- Why concentration and adaptability are vital

- The dangers of incorrect use of speed
- Why observation is important
- How to estimate speed
- The importance of weather and road conditions
- The importance of being safe on the road at all times.
-

C1:4 POSITIONING

The student should be able to:

Demonstrate the principles of correct positioning of the vehicle according to traffic conditions.

State the techniques and factors to be considered when positioning the vehicle on the road.

Key learning points

Supporting evidence is required of the students understanding of:

- How to position the vehicle safely according to traffic conditions
- Why forward vision is important
- The importance of assessing a potential hazard correctly
- How to position the vehicle safely when approaching a nearside junction
- The margins to be allowed between their vehicles and the vehicle in front and what factors effect that margin.

C1:5 CORNERS AND BENDS

The student should be able to:

Demonstrate, explain the importance of good corner and bend management.

Describe the basic techniques for achieving excellence.

Key learning points

Supporting evidence is required of the students understanding of:

- **The principles of cornering**
- **Why cornering correctly is important to the patient**
- **The safety factors when cornering**
- **About the forces affecting the vehicle and its passengers**
- **How vehicles condition affects cornering**
- **How road conditions affect stability when cornering**
- **How to approach a corner or turn.**

C1:6 OVERTAKING

The student should be able to:

Demonstrate the correct overtaking procedure.

Answer several relevant questions.

Key learning points

Supporting evidence is required of the students understanding of:

- Why overtaking with an ambulance poses special problems
- Occasions when a driver MUST NOT overtake
- The guidelines for overtaking safely
- Occasions when it is permissible to overtake
- The guidelines for overtaking safely
- Occasions when it is permissible to overtake on the left
- Why patients and erring on the side of safety are important
- The rules of overtaking.

C1:7 SKIDS

The student should be able to:

State the definition of skids

Describe the factors to minimise the risk of skidding.

Answer several relevant questions and on a skid training facility, recognise and correct the three types of skids.

Key learning points

Supporting evidence is required of the students understanding of:

- What a skid is and what features of the tyres may be involved
- What driving conditions cause a skid
- The road conditions which can present skid hazards
- How to drive to avoid skids
- Where counteracting skids can be practised
- What cadence braking is.

C1:8 NIGHT DRIVING

State the special demands night driving brings. Drive during the hours of darkness.

Key learning points

Supporting evidence is required of the students understanding of:

- What preparations to make before starting a driving night duty
- What you must check on your vehicle before driving at night

- What you must remember about your field of vision at night
- The causes of variations in available light at night and how you can help yourself cope with them
  - How to cope with dazzling headlights on other vehicles
  - How to deal with fatigue when you are driving at night.

C1: MOTORWAY DRIVING

The student should be able to:

List the three types of motorway. Describe the dangers of motorway driving. Discuss the various warning systems and what they mean. Drive on a motorway making safe progress, having regard to the high speeds encountered.

Key learning points

Supporting evidence is required of the students understanding of:
  - The purpose of motorways
  - The classes of road vehicles not allowed on motorways
  - The types of features of motorways found in the UK
  - How to join and leave a motorway safely
  - How to change lanes and overtake safely
  - What to do in fog
  - How to recognise and use emergency cross-over points
  - The precautions to take on elevated sections and bridges
  - Motorway signs/signals and their meanings
  - What to do if your vehicle breaks down
  - Overtaking procedures on motorways.

Glossary

APGAR - Appearance, Pulse, Grimace, Activity, and Respiration. A score is given to new-born babies to evaluate heath.

Aphasia – is the medical term used when someone has difficulty with speech or language.

Asystole – is demonstrated by a flat line on the ECG and is the most serious form of cardiac arrest. Adrenaline is given in an attempt to stimulate cardiac electrical activity. A flat line Asystole is not a shockable rhythm.

Atone – the undoing of sin, to make amends. Reparation.

Charismata - Spiritual gifts given by the Holy Spirit.

Crepitus – crepitus describes the cracking sound heard in joints moving and is used to describe bone ends rubbing against each other.

Decerebrate posturing – An ominous sign when muscles are tightened and held rigid, normally due to a brain injury. Arms and legs are held straight and the head and neck arch backwards.

Dextrocardia – dextrocardia is a rare congenital heart defect where the heart leans to the right instead of to the left.

ECMO - extracorporeal membrane oxygenation, ecmo for short is a machine that pumps blood outside the body to remove carbon dioxide. It is a form of life support.

EtOH – EtOH is Ethanol or ethyl alcohol and is a medical abbreviation used when someone is intoxicated by alcohol.

GCS – Glasgow Coma Scale is a scale used to measure someone's level of consciousness. 15 is normal and a GCS of 3 is deeply unconscious.

Hermeneutics – Interpretation of biblical texts. What did it mean when written and what does it mean today?

Hypoxia – this is a state where there is inadequate oxygen to the tissues and cells, potentially causing damage and organ failure or even death.

Intubation – the insertion of a tube into the trachea used to ventilate a patient.

IV – Intra venous

Laryngopharynx – the lower portion at the back of the throat through which, food, water and air passes.

Living will or advance care directive – this is a document that gives instruction about the medical care you wish to receive.

Opisthotonos – an abnormal posturing sometimes seen in traumatic death or when there is a serious brain injury/illness.

ROSC – the return of a spontaneous circulation. This indicates the outcome of pre-hospital response and intervention.

Rigor Mortis – rigor mortis is seen after death as the muscles and joints stiffen.

Moribund – moribund means at the point of death.

SpO2 – using a pulse oximeter measures SpO2 levels, which is the percentage of oxygen carried by the blood.

Parousia – this is a Greek word which simply means the second coming of Jesus.

PPCI – Primary Percutaneous Coronary Intervention, commonly called angioplasty, is a procedure to treat narrowed or blocked coronary arteries.

SCAS – South Central Ambulance Service.

MDT – Ambulance Mobile Data Terminal.

Paraesthesia – what we often call pins and needles.

TLoC - transient loss of consciousness.

Takotsubo – broken heart syndrome, thought to be caused by severe stress.

Trismus – locking of the jaw, making opening the mouth extremely difficult.

Tracheostomy – a surgical opening made through the neck into the windpipe.

References

Chapter 1

[1]Walter L. Bradley, PhD. Cited in Lee, Strobel. (2000). *The Case for Faith.* Grand Rapids, Michigan: Zondervan.

Chapter 2

https://albertmohler.com/2016/01/20/the-scandal-of-biblical-illiteracy-its-our-problem-4
[10]Atkinson, D. (2013 37). *The message of Genesis 1-11.* Nottingham, England: Inter-Varsity Press.
[3]Atkinson, D. (1994 35, 46-50). *Pastoral ethics. A guide to the key issues of daily living.* Oxford, England: Lynx Communications.
[2]Bell, R. (2007, 54). *Sex God. Exploring the endless connections between sexuality and spirituality.* Zondervan: Grand Rapids, Michigan.
[6]Bowie, R. (2004 90 190). *Ethical studies.* (Second edition). Cheltenham, United Kingdom: Nelson Thornes Ltd.
[12]Brown, D. (1991 110). *Choices. Ethics and the Christian.* Oxford, United Kingdom: Blackwell Publishers.
[13]Cairns, A. (1998 240-1) *Dictionary of Theological Terms.* (Second edition). Belfast: Ambassador-Emerald International.
[15]Fletcher, J. (1971 321). A dictionary of Christian ethics. In J. Macquarrie (Ed.), *Situation, situation ethics.* London, United Kingdom: SCM Press.
[11]Leal, D. (1996 11-12). *Debating homosexuality.* Cambridge, United Kingdom: Grove Books Limited.
[14]Mackinnon, D. M. (1971 351). A dictionary of Christian ethics. In J. Macquarrie (Ed.), *Utilitarianism.* London, United Kingdom: SCM Press.
[7]Messer, N. (2006 8). *Going by the book. The Bible and Christian ethics.* Norwich, United Kingdom: Canterbury Press.
NIV (2003). *The NIV Study Bible.* London: Hodder & Stoughton.
[16]Paul, I. (2014 25-26). *Same-sex unions. The key biblical texts.* Cambridge, United Kingdom: Grove Books Limited.
[4]Pigott, P. (2015). *BBC News. Lambeth diary: Anglicans in turmoil.* Retrieved from http://news.bbc.co.uk/1/hi/uk/7509125.stm
[9]Pollard, P. (1998 160-161). How does scripture speak to our lives? In G. Holloway, R. J. Harris & M. C. Black (Ed.). *Theology matters. Answers for the Church today.* Joplin, MO: College Press Publishing.

[8]Schuh, S. (2007). *Challenging Conventional Wisdom.* Retrieved from
http://www.courage.org.uk/articles/Challenging.shtml
[5]Smith, C. M. (1992 88-89). *Preaching as weeping, confession and resistance.
Radical responses to radical evil. Encountering handicappism, ageism, heterosexism,
sexism, white racism, classism.* Louisville, KY: Westminster/John Knox Press.

Chapter 5

[1] Gov.uk (2014) *The Mental Capacity Act code of practice.* Crown copyright.
[2]Health Professions Council (2008) Standards of conduct, performance
and ethics. Available at http://www.hpc-
uk.org/assets/documents/10002367FINALcopyofSCPEJuly2008.pdf
(accessed 23.05.09)
[3] NHS choices (2015). *Your health, your choices.* Retrieved from
https://nhs.uk/chq/Pages/899.aspx?CategoryID=68&SubCategoryID=1
56
[4] Eyre, H., Knight, R., & Rowe, G. (2009). *OCR religious studies. Philosophy
and ethics.* Harrow, United Kingdom: Heinemann.
[5]Atkinson, D, (1994). *Pastoral ethics. A guide to the key issues of daily living.*
Oxford, England: Lynx Communications.
[6]Veatch. R. M. (1997 378-379) *Medical ethics.* (Second edition). Mississauga,
Canada: Jones and Bartlett Publishers.
[7]Canton, N. L. (1993). *Advance directives and the pursuit of death with dignity.*
Dallas, TX: Indiana University Press.
[8]WHO - Preamble to the Constitution of the World Health Organization
as adopted by the International Health Conference, New York, 19-22
June, 1946; signed on 22 July 1946 by the representatives of 61 States
(Official Records of the World Health Organization, no. 2, p. 100) and
entered into force on 7 April 1948.
[9]Kubler-Ross (2003). *On Death and Dying* London: Tavistock Publications
Limited
[10] Mills, W. E. (1997). *Mercer dictionary of the Bible* Macon, GA: Mercer
University Press.
[11] Gushee, D. P. (2013). *The sacredness of human life. Why an ancient Biblical
vision is key to the world's future.* Grand Rapids, MI: Wm. B. Eerdmans
Publishing.
[12] McQuilkin, R., & Copan, P. (2014). *An introduction to biblical ethics.
Walking in the way of wisdom.* (Third edition). Downers Grove, IL: Inter
Varsity Press.
14   Atkinson, D, (1994, 219). *Pastoral ethics. A guide to the key issues of
daily living.* Oxford, England: Lynx Communications.

Chapter 6

[1]Phil Wickham – Living Hope
[2]The National Audit Office
http://www.nao.org.uk/system_pages/search.aspx?terms=dying+at+home+statistics+hospital (accessed 24.05.09).
[3]Clark, David. *"Palliative Care History: A Ritual Process."* European Journal of Palliative Care 7, no. 2 (2000):50-55
[4]Saunders, Cicely. *"Care of Patients Suffering from Terminal Illness at St. Joseph's Hospice,* Hackney, London.*"* Nursing Mirror, 14th February 1964
[5]Bowlby J: *Processes of mourning.* International Journal of Psychoanalysis 42: 317-340, 1961. Bowlby J: Attachment and Loss. vols. 1-3, New York: Basic Books, Inc., 1969-1980.
http://cancerweb.ncl.ac.uk/cancernet/306750.html (accessed 30.05.09)
[6]Parkes CM: *Bereavement: Studies of Grief in Adult Life.* 2nd ed., Madison: International Universities Press Inc., 1987. Parkes CM: Bereavement as a psychosocial transition: processes of adaptation to change. Journal of Social Issues 44(3): 53-65, 1988.
http://cancerweb.ncl.ac.uk/cancernet/306750.html (accessed 30.05.09)
[7]Dunn, J.E. (1975). *Jesus and The Spirit.* London: SCM Press.
[8]Stibbe, M. (2004). *Know your spiritual gifts.* (Second edition). Michigan: Zondervan.
[9]Pearson, M. (1995). *Christian Healing.* (Second edition). Lake Mary, FL 32746: Charisma House.
[10]Stanley, C. (1995). *The wonderful Spirit filled life.* Nashville, Tennessee: Thomas Nelson Publishers.
[11]Johnson, B., and Clark, R. (2011). *The essential guide to healing. Equipping all Christians to pray for the sick.* Minnesota: Chosen books.
[12]Cairns, A. (1998) *Dictionary of Theological Terms.* (Second edition). Belfast: Ambassador-Emerald International.
[13]Marshall, H., Travis, S., and Paul, I. (2011). *Exploring the New Testament. Volume 2. The Letters and Revelation.* (Second edition). London: Society for Promoting Christian Knowledge.
[14]Marx, M. (2008). *Healing on the streets. Training manual.* (Study pack). Causeway cost vineyard.
[15]Ogden, G. (2007). *Discipleship essentials. A guide to building your life in Christ.* (Expanded edition). Illinois: Inter-Varsity Press.
[15]Cantalamessa, R. (2003). *Come, creator Spirit. Meditations on the veni creator.* Minnesota: The Liturgical Press. NIV (2003). *The NIV Study Bible.* London: Hodder & Stoughton.

Chapter 9

[1]March on stress.com. (2015). *After an incident* (Booklet). Great Britain: March on Stress Ltd.

[2]TRiM by march on stress.com. (2015). *Trauma risk management. An organisational approach to personnel management in the wake of traumatic events.* Great Britain: March on Stress Ltd.

Chapter 10

[1]https://en.wikipedia.org/wiki/1979_in_the_United_Kingdom#:~:text= 1%20May%20%E2%80%93%20The%20London%20Underground,his% 20seat%20in%20the%20election.
[2]https://haemophilia.org.uk/public-inquiry/the-infected-blood-inquiry/the-contaminated-blood-scandal/ accessed 11.03.22
[3]**https://www.bbc.co.uk/news/uk-politics-39713396** NHS contaminated blood was 'criminal cover-up' – Burnham. (accessed 27.02.22).
[4]Tom Wright. *Surprised by HOPE.* Society for Promoting Christian Knowledge 2007

Chapter 11

[1]TRiM by march on stress.com. (2015). *Trauma risk management. An organisational approach to personnel management in the wake of traumatic events.* Great Britain: March on Stress Ltd.
[2]Brendon Hatmaker (2011-10-18) Barefoot Church: Serving the Least in a Consumer Culture (p.34) Zondervan.

Chapter 12

[1]Stranks. J. (2005 65). *Stress at Work. Management and Prevention.* Oxford: Elsevier Buterworth-Heinemann. [2]Independent Newspaper 7th November 2008 (page 28). See http://www.dailymail.co.uk/news/article-2272517/Stressed-ambulance-drivers-43-680-sick-days--40-rise-years.html
[3]Black, C., and Frost, D. (2011 55-58). *Health at work – an independent review of sickness absence.*

Chapter 13

[1]Tom Wright. *Surprised by HOPE.* Society for Promoting Christian Knowledge 2007
[2]Jim Caviezel testimony https://www.youtube.com/watch?v=vhDFwa69XVM 33:00 minutes
[3]Romans 10:9-10

Barbour, I. G. (1989-1991). *Ethics in an age of technology. The Gifford lectures. Volume two.* New York, NY: Harper Collins Publishers.

Behe, M. J., Dembski, W. A., Meyer, S. (2000). *Science and evidence for design in the universe. The proceedings of the Wethersfield institute. Volume 9.* San Francisco: Ignatius Press.

BBC. (2014). *History. Copernicus (1473-1543).* Retrieved from http://www.bbc.co.uk/history/historic_figures/copernicus.shtml

Bognar, G., and Hirose, I. (2014). *The ethics of healthcare rationing. An introduction.* Abingdon, UK: Routledge.

Collins, F. S. (2000, paragraph 70). *Religion and Ethics.* Retrieved from transcript of interview by Bob Abernethy with Francis Collins on PBS TV program. http://www.pbs.org/wnet/religionandethics/

Dawkins, R. (1994). *A lecture by Richard Dawkins extracted from The Nullifidian* Retrieved from http://www.thirdworldtraveler.com/Dawkins_Richard/NoNothings_Dawkins.html

Dawkins, R. (2006). *The God delusion.* Ealing, Great Britain: Transworld Publishers.

Eiseley, L.C. (1969). *Darwin's century. Evolution and the men who discovered it.* New York, NY: Doubleday.

Fee, G.W., Stuart, S. (2002). *How to read the Bible for all its worth.* (Second edition). Bletchley: Scripture Union.

Galilei, G. (2000). In Galli, M. & Olsen, T. (Ed.), *131 Christians everyone should know. From the editors of Christian history magazine* (p 355). Nashville, TN: Christianity Today.

Jacob's Ladder Ministry:
Web: Jacobsladderministry.co.uk
Email: jacobsladder55@outlook.com

Printed in Great Britain
by Amazon

19773134R00078